What Key People are ~~Saying about~~ Dr. Rhoberta Shaler's "Wrestling Rhinos: Conquering Conflict in the Wilds of Work"

"What a concept, "Wrestling Rhinos"! This book is needed in every business library. Rhoberta Shaler has distilled for you a wealth of specific recommendations to take the intimidation and anxiety out of your workdays. Conflict will always exist but those who can manage it well become masters of it, not victims."

Jim Cathcart, Author, *Relationship Selling*,
Lake Sherwood, CA   www.Cathcart.com

"It is common knowledge that the relationship a company has with its employees, and the rapport they have with each other, dramatically affects a firm's profitability. The organization that has excellent relations with its people will produce 40% more profits than those who don't. Yet most businesses do not have a program in place to maximize these assets. Do you?
Dr. Rhoberta Shaler brings this knowledge and expertise to the reader in this book as nobody else can. I strongly recommend you read it –and apply it–to your business. Your bottom-line will thank you!"

Allan S. Boress, CPA, CFE, Author, *The "I-Hate-Selling" Book*
www.AllanBoress.com, www.IHateSellingInstitute.com

"Dr. Shaler has put together a wonderful tutorial for all supervisors, managers and 'wannabe' managers in today's workforce. What impressed me most about the book, however, was how very relevant all of Shaler's teachings are outside the work place. These timely lessons apply to all of us in our personal lives as well—as parents, spouses, family, friends and neighbors."

David M. Brudney, ISHC, David Brudney & Associates
Hospitality Marketing Consultants, www.DavidBrudney.com

"Fasten your seatbelts! Here's a book that will put you on the fast-track of the Truth Train. It's not about waking up to smell the roses. It's waking up before you lose the rose bushes. Not just another intriguing book title, 'Wrestling Rhinos' will help you overcome both cultural and personal denials, contradictions, and avoidance in order to master those difficult to handle situations. I will recommend it to all of our readers— women leaders who have had to work harder than most to learn these principles. This book will make it much easier for all of us in the future!"

Pat Lynch, Founder and Editor in Chief, WomensRadio and WomensCalendar
www.WomensRadio.com, www.WomensCalendar.org

"Rhoberta Shaler's book is your personal coach, guiding you in all the right, productive directions with people. She is a master of negotiating results with, as she puts it, 'the person under that behavior who wants to be understood.'"

Mimi Donaldson, Co-author, *Negotiating for Dummies*
www.MimiSpeaks.com

"An instant classic! Dr. Shaler has delivered the only book that actually demonstrates how improving your people skills can lead to increased profits. Her sharp style and savvy examples clearly communicate how to turn this chronic problem into a powerful opportunity. Finally, a conflict management approach that's not as painful as the problem it attempts to solve! It may be a jungle out there, but with this fun-to-read guide you'll go from sticky situation to successful safari in no time. 'Wrestling Rhinos' is THE competitive edge for the 21st century. This year's must-read business title!"

Sterling Valentine, Marketing Expert
www.TurbochargeYourMarketing.com

"Many people work 40 hours a week or more, and conflicts can make it a very stressful experience. In 'Wrestling Rhinos: Conquering Conflict in the Wilds of Work', Dr. Rhoberta Shaler truly shares how people skills sharpen your competitive edge and how you can interact assertively with colleagues, clients, and bosses. She also reveals ideas on how to deal with anger, communication, competition, conflict, negotiation, and common sense. Transforming your outlook at the office will not only lessen conflicts in the workplace, it will also lead to a happier homelife. Written in Dr. Shaler's sincere, honest and appealing style, 'Wrestling Rhinos', is certainly an inspirational book and highly recommended for those that deal with these issues."

Roy Van Broekhuizen, CEO, www.OnlineTradingGuru.com

WRESTING RHINOS

Other books by Rhoberta Shaler, PhD

Optimize Your Day! Practical Wisdom for Optimal Living

Keep It In Mind: Memorable Messages for Staying on Track

What You Pay Attention To Expands: Focus Your Thinking. Change Your Results.

Upcoming titles:
The Universe Always Says 'Yes!' by Rhoberta Shaler, PhD

Walking in Mystery, Dancing in Wonder
by Rhoberta Shaler, PhD and G. Charles Andersen, MA

Wrestling RHINOS: CONQUERING CONFLICT in the WILDS OF WORK

RHOBERTA SHALER, PHD

People Skills Press • San Diego
www.OptimizeInstitute.com

Rhoberta Shaler, PhD
WRESTLING RHINOS: CONQUERING CONFLICT IN THE WILDS OF WORK
ISBN: 0-9711689-8-9

Edited by Kera McHugh
Cover design and book layout by
somethingelse web+graphics, www.time4somethingelse.com

"Rhobert" & "Rhonda" Rhino Illustrations © 2004 Conrad Schmidt, www.flashonshow.com
Cover photos & photo of Dr. Shaler © 2004 Joanna Herr, Herr Photography, Encinitas, CA
Rhino photographs © 2004 Matt Matthews (aka gpflman), Pittsburgh, PA.
Additional rhino photos courtesy of www.istockphoto.com

First Edition First Printing: 2005
Printed in the United States of America

Published by People Skills Press, San Diego CA

For information, contact:
Rhoberta Shaler, PhD
Optimize! Institute™, San Diego CA
Email: info@OptimizeInstitute.com
Website: www.OptimizeInstitute.com

❧   ❧   ❧

For all those who have left their footsteps for me to follow . . . and their footprints on my mind.

For those who have walked with me as we created and shared our stories and, especially. . .

For my best creative acts, Kera, Dirke and Paul.

Kera whose brilliant insights and generous spirit consistently put luster in my life, warmth in my heart, and, my words on the world.

Dirke whose strength and love of home and family consistently remind me what's important and fill me with pride.

Paul whose independence and conviction continuously teach me that unconditional love is my choice.

❧   ❧   ❧

≪ ≪ ≪

Without friends, life would be worth less. I have been so fortunate to share love and life with wonderful, interesting, empathetic, challenging, supportive, stimulating, honest, forthright family, friends and colleagues. I want to both acknowledge and thank you all. Through our journey together, we have shared our stories, our joys, our victories, our sorrows, our disappointments, our insights and our challenges, and for that I am grateful daily.

≪ ≪ ≪

INSIDE THIS BOOK:

RHINO RAMPAGES:
MANAGING CONFLICT WITHOUT LOSING CO-WORKERS, CLIENTS, CREDIBILITY, OR SLEEP

RHINO RAGE: MANAGING ANGER: DON'T TELL ME TO CALM DOWN!

RHINO WRANGLING:
NEGOTIATING SKILLS THAT GET YOU WHAT YOU WANT

RULES, REMNANTS & RUMINATIONS:
UNCOMMON COMMON SENSE FOR WORKING WELL TOGETHER

A good manager doesn't try to eliminate conflict; he tries to keep it from wasting the energies of his people. If you're the boss and your people fight you openly when they think that you are wrong—that's healthy.

Robert Townsend

Integrate what you believe into every single area of your life. Take your heart to work and ask the most and best of everybody else, too.

Meryl Streep

WHY RHINOS?

Rhinoceros are often portrayed as aggressive and unintelligent but that is not their true nature. They simply *cannot* see. That's the case with "rhino" people as well. They simply *do not* see. They do not see any other ways to behave, interact, solve problems, or to make their pain go away. So, they lash out in one way or another.

Rhinos at work—and at home—have many ways to make their point. They may be overbearing, aggressive or generally grumpy. Each behavior is aimed at increasing their sense of control. They want acknowledgment for their opinion, or their superiority. They may be unresponsive, ignoring your presence . . . until they feel threatened. Then they surprise you with a ferociousness that seems completely out of proportion to your proximity.

In the real rhinoceros world, things are more clear. When neighboring rhinos meet, one of them must become subordinate or violence is likely. If that doesn't happen, say, by one turning back its ears, the stage is set for a contest that can quickly turn violent. Have you met workplace rhinos who behave exactly the same way? You may have been totally unaware that you had compromised their turf. Their hyper-vigilance for intruders is remarkable and their response, unpredictable. And, then, they charge when your back is turned!

Both male and female rhinos are aggressive and possessive. They will both fight for their land due to their extreme territoriality. Before their famed "bull charge" rhinos will lower their heads, scream and paw the earth at a distance to demonstrate their courage . . . and, no doubt, to summon it as well. If the intruder does not retreat, the defender will charge, hopefully sending the alien to the other side of the savannah with its tail between its legs, licking its wounds and knowing its place.

When rhinos collide, they seem to test each other's bravery with force, loud snorts, and thunderous pawing of the ground designed to cause the other to retreat. Failure of one to back down produces a stand-off. Each lowers its head and readies its horns. They charge, attempting to pierce the sides of their antagonist and draw blood. Rhinos will lock horns and try to push each other backwards. You've likely experienced this phenomena with someone at work. In an instance like this, the rhino with the greater strength and positioning will be victorious. Fortunately, even with their great strength and extreme ferociousness, they do not battle to the death. The loser simply retreats, usually with plans of revenge at a later time. Sound familiar?

I was working with a coaching client (we'll call her Sylvia) who had been recently promoted to the executive suite, where there were eight people already in positions of power. She met her rhino on her first day upstairs. When introduced, the rhino (let's call him Joe) stood a little too close, crushed Sylvia's hand a little too long, and smiled only from the nose down. Sylvia knew immediately that they failed to share a definition of *team*. Joe's non-verbal horn-locking with the desire to push Sylvia backwards was clear. He wanted her to know who he thought was the king of the beasts in that jungle.

Wisely, Sylvia smiled, looked into Joe's eyes, extracted her hand from his grip, and said:

"I'm looking forward to working with you, Joe. Being asked
to join this executive team is an exciting opportunity and I'm
sure we'll find many ways to work well together. Let's sit
down soon and learn more about each other."

No threatening behavior from her. She could *see*. The rhino had nothing
to react against and he turned and went back to his grass. Had Sylvia
challenged Joe, the posturing might have continued. Had she questioned his
mixed message, she might have set herself up as his own personal target. She
did nothing but stand firm and express openness. A great beginning!

Would you have stood your ground when you were standing on someone
else's dung heap?

In the wild, a rhinoceros defends its turf vigorously against rivals. Rhinos
don't see well. In contrast, they do have highly developed senses of smell and
hearing. This combination allows them to operate only on limited input, and
on assumption and deduction. Dangerous!

They can see clearly for only a very short distance in front of themselves.
Therefore, they simply do not (cannot?) see the big picture. Imagine their
distress when someone wants to paint it for them and fill in their blanks.
They must say no, because a larger scheme of things does not exist for them.
In fact, it represents something scary and beyond their control. What to do?
Get it out of the way. Reduce the risk. Stop the threat. Charge!

You may know the phrase from Abraham Maslow,

"When all you have is a hammer, you tend to see everything
as a nail."

Office rhinos (ORs) have this problem. Their limited sensory perception,
combined with lack of skills, and lack of insight too, they hammer away at
anything that looks like a threat.

The rhinoceros is a solitary animal. Did they become solitary because they
chased away all folks, friendly or otherwise? Or, were they naturally solitary
. . . preferring to stay that way and thus chasing away all who would come
close? Who knows?

Rhinos are never seen in large groups. They only become somewhat
tolerant of others at the watering hole. There they are simply too thirsty to
pay attention to others and there is a degree of respect for privacy. Of course,

rhinos also become friendlier during mating season. (We'll leave the topic of harassment for another time!)

Rhinos have been around since the Miocene era millions of years ago. They have their stories. so do office rhinos. The truth is that work is not the place to uncover childhood issues, nor is it to be expected that folks will make allowances for those unresolved issues. ORs make their own beds. If they happen to own the savannah you are working on, beware. There may be little you can do. It's their turf, after all. If, however, they are simply behaving *as though* they own the turf, your skills can have a great impact.

Now, about that watering hole. Every rhino stakes out a territory that includes a watering hole and a mud wallow. Interesting, isn't it, how they like to control the resources? It gives them a sense of power, even if it is over office supplies. They keep an eye on where folks gather. Some like to dominate the landscape, while others prefer to watch from a distance.

Most rhinos are gentle and timid when left alone. They will just go about their business until something startles them. In the wild, rhinos startle easily . . . at about thirty feet. That's quite a large comfort zone! Once someone steps within it, even though the intruder cannot be seen, it is heard and smelled. Alert! Alert! There is something to fear. Hyper-vigilance ensues until the decision is made to relax or charge. And, rhinos will charge with great ferocity very little provocation. In fact, often without a reason at all.

At work, you've likely had an experience like that. You've been working with someone who you seem to have an easy, collaborative relationship with on a day-to-day basis. No problems. Then, a new animal walks on to the savannah, challenges the turf . . . or, simply walks by on the way to the watering hole, and WHAM! Uncertain as to the purpose of the intruder, all the warning bells go off and the OR is at the ready. Defenses are mustered. Offenses prepared. "Nothing will sneak up on me and challenge my territory," s/he thinks. Charge!

The unsuspecting antelope with only water on his mind is cut down on the way to the water cooler. He's skewered, thrust into the air and trampled before he knows he's stepped over the line.

The size of a rhino's home range can differ according to its sex, its age or the type of habitat it prefers. The more immature ones usually occupy larger areas than the adults. The only time they actually gather in groups is temporarily to wallow. Can't you just see a group of young executives gathered at their local watering hole, wallowing in the triumphs and thrusts of the day? Rhino behavior? Could be.

Now, before we start thinking of rhinos only as *them*, it is important to note that every one of us is a potential rhino. We may not behave like rhinos as a rule, BUT, we definitely have the ability to be startled and charge at inopportune moments. We may be head-down, tail-up in our work and oblivious to our surroundings when an enthusiastic co-worker breaks our concentration or interrupts our flow. Rhino rage may erupt. A rhino rant spills from our lips . . . and we do not even recognize ourselves for a moment or two. It happens. **Each person is someone else's idea of a rhino at some time!**

You've had your moments, too. Remember this truth as it helps with perspective when you can see and someone else cannot. Back off and regain your vision. Ask a co-worker to give you a Rhino Report—the straight goods on how you're behaving—and agree to do the same for her. This way, Rhino Rampages, Rants and Rages can be stopped before the acceleration to "Full Speed Charge" is engaged.

Rhinos do not kill things on purpose. They simply want their fear to go away and for the world to leave them alone. If you were new to the jungle, could not see, and had to rely on your senses of smell and hearing, would you be a little paranoid? Your job is to create vision and safety for rhinos if you need or want to share their savannahs and watering holes. They may not own that property but they have a great need to control it. When you think you own something, you strive to hang on to it. When you can't see the big picture, the thought of losing what you *can* see is frightening. Helen Keller said,

> "The most pathetic person in the world is someone who has sight, but has no vision."

Rhinos may not be pathetic, but the fear they experience when they feel threatened is real. It renders them ineffective, yet offensive; a time and energy wasting condition that retards growth, progress, and team synergy. Remember, too, that despite size (physical or personality wise) rhinos are surprisingly light on their feet and able to turn on a dime and start off in another direction as easily as a polo pony. You might try to see your way clearly to understand their blindness and realize their need for safety. Could you make a little extra room for your ORs? Could you offer to point them in the right direction and turn their formidable strength towards a positive goal?

It is within your power when it is within your skill set.

Should we have to accommodate these beasts? Should every day be a "rhino wrestling" day? Rhino wrestling makes life difficult. It makes the workplace challenging and it makes joy harder to maintain. What are the alternatives? If you do not have the skills, insights and strategies to wrestle rhinos effectively, you have two choices: be miserable, anxious and stressed, or be constantly looking for work until you own your own savannah.

Rhinos come in all sizes at all levels in the organization. One might surprise you in the mail room, the cafeteria, the staff lounge, the executive suite or the board room. They are everywhere. You need to be properly equipped to wrestle!

This book has three purposes:

- ⊕ **To help you understand the rhino within,**

- ⊕ **To teach you to become an intrepid intruder when nudges are necessary and,**

- ⊕ **To give you the attitudes and insights, skills and strategies to confidently wrestle rhinos for productivity, profit and peak performance!**

Don't let a little skirmish ruin your day.
Become a Resourceful Rhino Wrestler!

IS THERE A RHINO IN YOUR OFFICE?

You'll know, for sure, if there's a rhino in your office. They are irritating, overwhelming, and sometimes loud. They take attention away from more important matters and they make a mess wallowing in their own mud. Rhinos create uproar, uncertainty, and definitely conflict. Conflict, though, to some degree, is a daily reality that rhinos add to enormously.

Many people may be quite ready to talk *about* the rhino but never talk *to* the rhino. Some people get pre-occupied by their fear, disgust, or frustration with ORs and productivity slows. Tempers flare and mountains are made of molehills all over the place. Other folks cower when faced with rhinos and work hard to avoid them at all costs. And still others seem to enjoy making the rhinos charge. Denying the presence of rhinos in your office is a dangerous practice. None of these approaches solve the problem. Rhinos need to be seen, heard . . . and handled!

Folks try to pretend the rhino is not there in a vain hope that it will not be real or will disappear if ignored. Not so! Everyone notices and everyone's productivity suffers. How can you work when you're busy pussyfooting around a rhinoceros?

Basically, whenever your needs or values come into opposition with those of others, conflict can result. Some conflicts are minor and relatively easy to handle. Some can be avoided completely with a little skill and finesse. Others are of greater magnitude and must be tactically and truthfully addressed or they will escalate. Some conflicts cannot be resolved, but, they can and must *be managed.*

Do you feel competent, comfortable and confident about your conflict management skills? Not many people do. Conflict brings up bad memories, reminding you of fear rejection, pain, or feeling small. Our instinct is to run away, to avoid rather it than resolve it! A drastic measure that is all too common is leaving a job. If unresolved conflict is causing you to consider that option, learn to manage conflict—even before it starts. That's what communication skills are for! The rhinos are real! It is a big mistake to tiptoe around them and try to keep them from seeing you. Changing jobs won't give you the skills. It will leave you wanting to change jobs again at the next sign of conflict. Do you need that stress?

Rhinos are territorial and they like to keep a big area for themselves. They will charge anything that enters their domain. They ask neither permission nor forgiveness because they are simply doing all that they know to do to protect themselves. The rhino doesn't hate the man or jeep it's charging at. It simply wants to keep itself safe and its territory protected. This is true of the office rhinos as well. Since there is more likelihood of running into a rhino of the office variety, the risk is high. There are ways to reduce the risk.

A FEW BASIC IDEAS WILL GET US IN TRAINING TO BE RADICAL RHINO WRESTLERS

✧ **Get the best communication, conflict, and anger management skills you can.** Training is readily available so there is no excuse for not equipping yourself well and practicing daily. Communication skills come first. It is essential to be able to convey your thoughts, feelings, beliefs, and wants in clear, concise ways. And, you must be an active, aware listener. Remember, there is a very good reason why you have two ears and only one mouth!!!

⊕ **Bellowers lose.** All that noise drives folks away. It does, however, warn you of a "Rhino Crossing" so that you can get out of the way.

⊕ **Be aware of *your* values and needs, as well as those of others.** If you value timeliness and punctuality, it may be hard to work with someone who does not. But if they are still getting the job done and not interfering with your success, your judgment of them would be practically unfounded. Even though you may be annoyed by their behavior, there would not be evidence that it is affecting the quality of their work. If, on the other hand, their behavior was making it difficult, or even impossible, for you to complete your work on time, the issue would have to be named, claimed, and tamed.

⊕ **Have a values discussion with your coworkers.** Get important considerations on the table. Talk about possible implications and scenarios of differing values. Make a plan to manage those situations long before they become an issue.

How do you manage when a situation that seemed good starts to go wrong? Use these steps:

Name It!

This is the first and often the most difficult step. Be willing and able to say,

> "I did not receive the reports I needed on time in order to meet my deadline."

Simply and clearly *giving the issue a name* is the beginning of resolving it. After you declare the issue, do not fill in the blank space following it that is so tempting. This will take some effort on your part as you may want to appear understanding or make the other person feel better. You may even want to fill in (or make up) possible reasons why the other person did not do their part. Resist the urge!

Claim It!

The most important thing is to *own the issue as yours*, for example,

> "When *I* do not receive the reports I need on time, I cannot meet my deadlines. When that happens, I feel (angry, embarrassed, incompetent, frustrated, annoyed, irritated, helpless). I like to meet my commitments and get things done on time."

Now you have clearly taken ownership of the event and your feelings about it. You have laid no blame but have simply stated the issue and its effect on you.

Tame It!

You began this conversation with hope of finding a collaborative solution. You want the help of your colleague(s), so, ask for it!

> "Can we make an agreement to stick to our timelines and deliver so that things work well for everyone? In order to do this, are there any factors (obstacles, unforeseen circumstances) that we may have to handle first? Are there any major hurdles that we have to overcome?"

Then, seriously and respectfully, listen and work together on solutions. Be as specific as possible. Decide what will happen if the new agreement is broken. Agreement at this stage is essential.

Lead It Away!

Be sure to thank folks for listening and for their willingness to cooperate in managing *your* issue. With this approach, you are offering a strategy for problem-solving that others may also use. This contributes positively to your corporate culture.

Remember, an un-talked-about issue is like having a rhinoceros in your office. It is taking up space, coming between people, and making the atmosphere generally unpleasant. An untamed rhino can charge unpredictably at any minute.

Give it a name. Claim it, tame it and lead it away!

It's a lot less messy and takes much less energy than walking around it and cleaning up after it daily!

LIKE A RHINOCEROS

Renouncing violence
for all living beings,
harming not even a one,
you would not wish for offspring,
    so how a companion?

Wander alone, like a rhinoceros.
For a sociable person
there are allurements;
on the heels of allurement, this pain.
Seeing allurement's drawback,
wander alone, like a rhinoceros.

One whose mind
is enmeshed in sympathy
for friends & companions,
neglects the true goal.
Seeing this danger in intimacy,
wander alone, like a rhinoceros . . .

If you gain a mature companion,
    a fellow traveler, right-living & wise,

overcoming all dangers
    go with him, gratified,
    mindful.

If you don't gain a mature companion,
    a fellow traveler, right-living & wise,
        go alone
    like a king renouncing his kingdom,
    like the elephant in the Matanga wilds,
        his herd.

We praise companionship
    -- yes!
Those on a par, or better,
should be chosen as friends.
If they're not to be found,
    living faultlessly,
wander alone, like a rhinoceros.

Seeing radiant bracelets of gold,
well-made by a smith,
    clinking, clashing,
    two on an arm,
wander alone, like a rhinoceros,

[Thinking:] "In the same way,
if I were to live with another,
there would be careless talk or abusive."
Seeing this future danger,
wander alone, like a rhinoceros.

Because sensual pleasures,
elegant, honeyed, & charming,
bewitch the mind with their manifold forms -- seeing
this drawback in sensual strands --
wander alone, like a rhinoceros.

"Calamity, tumor, misfortune,
disease, an arrow, a danger for me."
Seeing this danger in sensual strands,
    wander alone, like a rhinoceros . . .

Avoid the evil companion
    disregarding the goal,
    intent on the out-of-tune way.
Don't take as a friend
someone heedless & hankering.
Wander alone, like a rhinoceros.

Consort with one who is learned,
  who maintains the Dhamma,
  a great & quick-witted friend.
Knowing the meanings,
subdue your perplexity,
[then] wander alone, like a rhinoceros . . .

Unstartled,   like a lion at sounds.
Unsnared,   like the wind in a net.
Unsmeared,   like a lotus in water:
wander alone, like a rhinoceros . . .

At the right time consorting
with the release through good will,
      compassion,
      appreciation,
      equanimity,
unobstructed by all the world,
    any world,
wander alone, like a rhinoceros.

Having let go of passion,
      aversion,
      delusion;
having shattered the fetters;
undisturbed at the ending of life,
wander alone, like a rhinoceros.

People follow & associate
  for a motive.
Friends without a motive these days
  are rare.
They're shrewd for their own ends, & impure.
  Wander alone, like a rhinoceros

- Theravedic Text

Skill in the art of communication is crucial to a leader's success. He can accomplish nothing unless he can communicate effectively.

Norman Allen

RHINO WRESTLING:

PEOPLE SKILLS TO SHARPEN YOUR COMPETITIVE EDGE

**You mustn't mess me about. I know I
may seem like a rhinoceros, but really,
I have thin skin.**

Minnie Driver, "Circle of Friends"

USE PEOPLE SKILLS TO SHARPEN YOUR COMPETITIVE EDGE

What is your competitive edge? Where is it found? It's not on your balance sheet. A profit is only the *evidence* of a competitive edge. The edge itself is found in your relationships.

Your business *is* the "people" business. Every business is. Certainly you have products, skills, expertise, and experience to offer, but first you need the people. There is no business without them.

- People *are* the economy. It is people you respond to and prepare for
- People have needs and wants
- People create competition and cooperation
- People create demands and expectations, timelines and deadlines, urgencies and emergencies
- People make or break a business

To sharpen your competitive edge, you must hone your people skills. *Excellent people skills build trusting relationships.* These are essential to your bottom line. Whether you are relating to folks you work with, work for, or live with, the better your skills the more likely the relationship will be productive and satisfying. Honing your skills, then, makes ultimate sense. It will save you time, energy, fear, and pain. What a bargain!

We know our world has speeded up. We have changed our sense of time and urgency. Do you remember when the mail and the telephone were the primary modes of business communication? Fast forward! Have you ever sent an e-mail and rushed back to your computer three minutes later expecting a reply? Were you annoyed when it was not there? Would you think of waiting for a document to arrive in the mail when there is a fax machine close at hand?

We live in an new era of instant communication with a desire for instant gratification. If we blink, we're afraid we'll miss something. If we slow down, we're afraid we'll be passed. If we stop, we're afraid we'll be too far out of the loop to regain our place. Our radar is always on. It's exhausting.

To live and work comfortably, we need to develop and refine our people skills. This will protect our own sanity as well as contributing to our business success.

How do you increase your business, improve workplace and client relationships, AND keep your health and sanity—simultaneously?

- ✦ Define clear goals
- ✦ Establish priorities
- ✦ Develop excellent people skills
- ✦ Be organized
- ✦ Manage time thoughtfully, and
- ✦ Be in integrity with all those things at all times

Simple to say but not always easy to do!

FOUR ESSENTIAL SKILLS TO SHARPEN YOUR COMPETITIVE EDGE:

BE ASSERTIVE, NOT AGGRESSIVE

Be clear. Know what you want AND why you want it. Know what is important to you and why. Then you will be able to communicate assertively and respectfully.

Your success will be in direct proportion to your clarity. Assertiveness means being willing to ask for what you need and want. Assertiveness requires that you speak about yourself, your thoughts, your feelings, your needs and wants. It is a declaration of where you stand. It is not an opportunity to step on or over others. That is aggressiveness. Big difference!

Assertive people communicate in ways which "enable them to maintain self-respect, pursue happiness and the satisfaction of their needs while defending their rights and personal space without abusing or dominating other people."[1] So writes Robert Bolton in his excellent book, *People Skills.* Aggressive people, on the other hand, express their feelings, needs, and ideas at the expense of others. It is difficult to feel safe around aggressive people, as they are often behaving from fear and insecurity. They also tend to be unpredictable.

Practice assertiveness.

COMMUNICATE CLEARLY

Communication involves two separate and distinct acts:

- ✦ The *willingness and ability to listen*
- ✦ The *willingness and ability to convey your message clearly*

One is more difficult than the other. Any guesses?

Why is it so difficult to listen well when we all long to be understood? We are impatient. Instead of listening when another person is speaking, we are formulating our answer, defense, or rebuttal in our heads. This precludes listening. We are fearful, too. We are concerned that we will not be understood and so we grab as much airtime for ourselves as possible. This also precludes listening *well*.

Robert Bolton says that,

> "75% of oral communication is ignored, misunderstood, or quickly forgotten. Rarer still is the ability to listen for the deepest meanings in what people say."[2]

It is rare, in part, because it is scary. If you really listen to someone, you have to become more deeply involved in the relationship if only for the length of the conversation. It's scary, too, because once you *do* understand the speaker, you may have to take action!

Listening requires caring. I have to *want* to listen. I have to be *willing* to ask questions that will help me better understand the speaker's point of view.

Now, for the other side of the equation. Speakers need to choose their words carefully to convey their message to the listener. They need to use language the listener understands. Both parties in a conversation must engage for communication to occur. It is a shared responsibility.

Remember, you can say a great deal without speaking. Body language is powerful . . . and it can be misread. Behavior often screams. What do you communicate when you do not attend a meeting? When you do not return a phone call? Are you aware of all the messages you are sending?

Leave nothing to chance that is within your control to communicate clearly.

Com-mun-i-ca-tion, n. an act or instance of transmitting; a verbal or written message; a process by which information is exchanged between individuals; personal rapport; a technique for expressing ideas effectively.

Com-mun-i-cate, vb. to convey knowledge of or information about; make known; to reveal by clear signs; to cause to pass from one to another; to transmit information, thought, or feeling so that it is satisfactorily received or understood.[3]

Big Difference!

To communicate is to use much more than words. To communicate takes not one interchange but many. Listen well and state the essence of what you heard. It is neither parroting nor paraphrasing, but rather continuing the conversation by listening for the clear intention conveyed in the message. Reflect more than the words. Check for the accuracy of the whole message— the feelings, beliefs, and values beneath the words. It's a risk worth taking. You are going for true understanding.

MANAGE CONFLICT PRODUCTIVELY

Conflict is not a four-letter word! It is simply the expression of opposing needs, drives, wishes, or demands. The challenge is how conflict is managed . . . or, if it is managed at all.

Assertive people can manage conflict more productively than passive or aggressive folks. Assertive people clearly communicate their positions and support them with their thoughts. They contribute to the conversation rather than create chaos.

Many people have had very poor experiences with conflict. It is not uncommon for conflict to be equated with disrespect. That is, of course, because of the awkward ways in which conflict is often handled.

The first step in managing conflict productively is to *clarify the issue for yourself.*

   ✦   Is it a conflict of emotions or feelings about something?

   ✦   Is it a conflict of values?

   ✦   Or is it a conflict of needs?

These are very different. Conflicts of emotions are the easiest to resolve. Why? Because we create our own feelings by what we choose to perceive and think, and these feelings can be changed. I may feel very strongly about something and you may be feeling completely the opposite. We are each entitled to our feelings, and once we have explained our feelings we can understand one another better . . . especially if we were really listening.

We may agree to disagree. Conflicts of values or needs are more complex. They will take longer to explain, understand, and manage. If you value the relationship, be willing to take the time.

It is essential to be *respectful when conflict is present*. When fear rises, defensiveness and attack often rise as well. **Take care to avoid piling hurt upon conflict.**

Anger is an arousal in the body created by hurt, fear, or frustration (or a combination of those.) When anger flares, it is a poor time to converse. Physiologically, the angrier a person becomes the poorer their ability to think becomes. Haven't we all experienced saying exactly what we will most regret at moments of intense anger? That's because as anger rises, the blood rushes from the centers of reason and logic in the brain out to the body to protect the vital organs. So, in a sense, the angrier you are, the more brain-dead you become. Not a good time for a conversation!

Learn the skills of assertion. Clarify your thoughts and approach people with whom you have conflict at a quiet time, not when you are in full flight, gun loaded, and out for bear!

ENGAGE IN TEAM PROBLEM-SOLVING

Or, "**Communicate. Communicate. Communicate.**" Whenever challenges arise in organizations or in families, the best approach is to move towards one another. Yet the tendency is often to move away. That's fear again. Or, the ostrich syndrome. Developing the skills of communication makes everyone's jobs easier.

Take the time to define the problem carefully. Often there is a tendency to make assumptions and leap to problem-solving before the problem itself is understood. Ask each team member for a statement of the issue. Discuss these fully and come to agreement about the nature of the challenge.

Know what you want the outcome or solution to accomplish. In the software industry, this would be *defining the requirements*. "What do we want to have, to feel, to 'be able to do', as a result of this effort?"

Once the problem or challenge and the desired goal are defined, choose the path to achieving the goal.

- ✦ Discuss it fully.
- ✦ What are the implications for every team member?
- ✦ How will this detract from other current projects?

✦   What are the priorities?

✦   Who will do what by when?

Create a linear plan with input from everyone involved. Decide on regular times to review and evaluate the progress and process. This saves time and unnecessary work. It keeps the challenge shared and maintains focus.

By honing these four essential people skills, you will feel more confident when you move into new relationships and more comfortable managing and strengthening existing ones.

Successful people and successful organizations focus on their goals, objectives, and plans. Successful relationships are the cornerstones of successful businesses.

Lasting relationships are built on honesty, integrity, skills, and the intention to learn. The trust created will lead everyone concerned to profit in every way.

1. Robert Bolton, *People Skills: How to Assert Yourself, Listen to Others, and Resolve Conflicts.* (New York: Simon & Schuster, 1979.)
2. Ibid.
3. *Webster's Ninth New Collegiate Dictionary.* (Springfield, Mass: Merriam-Webster, Inc. 1989)

It's useless to put your best foot forward—and then drag the other.

Anonymous

ARE YOU PUTTING YOUR BEST FOOT FORWARD?

W hat does it take to put your best foot forward? How do you present yourself in the best light possible? Why would you want to?

The expression "to put your best foot forward" came from colonial times when, to impress a woman at a dance, a man would step forward to display his more muscular calf, or put forward his best foot. We do not only put our best foot forward to impress others but also to feel good about ourselves. No one feels good, no matter what they say to the contrary, when they present or represent themselves poorly. You feel energized when you shine up real nice, don't you?

I'm not speaking only about physical appearance, although that is usually the way most folks make their first impression. In her book *Put Your Best Foot Forward*, Jo-Ellan Demetrius says there are seven ways in which we make an impression on others, first or otherwise.[1] Let's take a look at how to manage those impressions to ensure that they serve us well.

|||||||||||||||||||||||||||||||||||||||||||||||||||||||||||||||||||||||||||||||||||||||||||||||||||||||||||||||||||||||||||||||||||||

APPEARANCE

In many, many instances, the first impression you make is through your physical appearance. Have you taken the time to look your best? Are you dressed appropriately? Is your hair clean and shiny and your breath fresh? It may seem pretentious, to some, to consciously consider those things beforehand, but the fact is, they matter. The second, but equally important, aspect of your appearance is your body language. You display your gestures and stance, and other people attribute meaning to them consciously or unconsciously. You may be extremely competent at your work and yet have a mousy demeanor. What kind of information will first reach folks? Is your body language open or closed? Do you usually keep your arms folded across your chest or grasped like a fig leaf in front of you? This is closed body language and sends a message that you feel threatened, challenged or defensive. You are unconsciously protecting your vital organs from attack. Is this the message you wish to send?

VOICE

What does your voice convey? A reader once asked how to change her voice to sound more professional. It was a welcome question as many folks are not aware of the effect of their speaking voice on others. Is your voice calm, confident, compassionate, sexy, harsh, shrill, soft? As you hear a person's voice, you form stronger impressions of his or her personality, don't you? Tape record your voice and listen for the message of the voice, regardless of the words. This is an important consideration for you.

COMMUNICATION STYLE

What is your communication style?

- ✦ Do you ask questions or pontificate?
- ✦ Do you listen carefully or begin speaking before the other person is finished?
- ✦ Do you answer questions directly or beat around the bush?

✧ Do you volunteer information or withhold it?

✧ Are you blunt or evasive?

✧ Are you argumentative or compliant?

These are some important questions posed by Demetrius. Regardless of the content of your communication, your style speaks volumes.

CONTENT OF COMMUNICATION

What do you have to say? Your vocabulary is an indicator of your familiarity with your language. When you are just learning a new language, it is amazing how much you can communicate with just two hundred words. When you are speaking in your first language, though, it is amazing how much you can communicate if you *do not* use more than two hundred words!

How do you express your thoughts? Do you offer good information and food for thought or do you ramble on to fill space? Of course, different folks have different communication styles for differing places and relationships. That's a given. For now, look at your general way of expressing your thoughts. Is it engaging or boring? Is it respectful? Can it be understood by the listeners? You are not communicating when you speak over the heads of folks. Even Einstein said:

> "Everything should be made as simple as possible—but no simpler".

Be sure to use shared language if you truly want to communicate rather than just speak!

ACTIONS

Here's where the rubber hits the road! What does your behavior say about you? There is little point in saying that respect is a key value for you if you rush to push through a door ahead of others, demand your dinner first, or arrive late to meetings on a regular basis.

How do you treat strangers?

- ✦ Do you make everyone you meet feel special and worthy of your attention?
- ✦ Do you have double standards?
- ✦ Do you take action rather than talk about things?
- ✦ Do you walk your talk?
- ✦ Are you fair?
- ✦ Do you catch folks doing things right?
- ✦ Do you hog the credit for accomplishments even when your contribution was minimal?

When I was working with couples in relationship counseling, one partner would usually offer,

"But, I love him/her."

My question was always,

"What behaviors do you have that would consistently convey that message to your partner?"

This same scenario applies in the workplace. Look carefully at your behavior. What you do speaks very loudly.

ENVIRONMENT

- ✦ What do you surround yourself with?
- ✦ Who do you spend your time with?
- ✦ Is your lifestyle congruent with the things you say matter to you?
- ✦ How do you maintain your personal spaces?
- ✦ Is your home or office efficient, functional and practical, or artistic, fun and creative?
- ✦ What do you keep or display in your space?
- ✦ How does your space smell?

Folks are affected by those things. There's a *Lexus* ad that reads simply: "It also functions like a resume." That's a powerful observation. Whether this *should* be true or not, you know the way the world works. Your personal environment indicates many unspoken things about you. If you say you value organization but your office is a danger zone, what will people believe? Take the time and effort make your surroundings match what you say and do.

YOUR CHOICES

Your approach to life will be demonstrated in all these ways. Some you may agree with, others you may not, however, folks are watching. They will apply their criteria whether or not you want them to.

Of course, you do not live to meet the standards of others. You live to meet your own. The point is: you have the opportunity to control how you present yourself, and whether or not what you say matches what you do. This congruence is the basis of your integrity.

- ⊕ What are you communicating?
- ⊕ Are you communicating those things consciously?
- ⊕ If you're not getting the results you want or expect, take a closer look at the ways you make impressions and adjust accordingly.

Once your communication is conscious and intentional, you can rest assured that you have carefully chosen the results.

**Are you putting your best foot forward,
or could you use a shine?**

1. Jo-Ellan Demetrius. *Put Your Best Foot Forward.* (New York: Scribner, 2000).

Conflict is inevitable, but combat is optional.

Anonymous

WHAT'S YOUR BASIC M.O.—
PASSIVE, AGGRESSIVE,
OR ASSERTIVE?

Passive, aggressive or assertive. Can you choose wisely in any given situation? As with conflict management skills, we need a wide range of options when choosing the appropriate behavior for any situation.

There are times when we do not have a strong or pressing need for things to go a particular way. We can be passive. When a bear is grabbing at our children, aggression is best. Generally, assertiveness is most effective. It offers the most direct, clear, and appropriate avenue for expressing your wants, needs, and desired outcomes. It's that simple!

If you do not have the full menu of skills and the full repertoire of responses, you are cheating yourself. Even when you have no particularly strong desire or opinion about something, you need the skills to express that effectively, which requires assertiveness. Otherwise, your response can be interpreted as "wishy-washy," gutless, or inconsequential. Who would risk that? Assertiveness demonstrates that you value yourself. Would you want to do anything less?

PASSIVE BEHAVIOR

Being passive is the easy way out with the least amount of friction and the highest personal cost. Now, there's a real bargain!

Passive behavior may appeal to you because it usually allows you to avoid, postpone, ignore, or mask your feelings in any potentially conflicting situation. But, do you respect yourself in the morning? No, because you did not respect yourself enough to say what was on your mind. (Ah, the rhino within.) This habit is damaging to your self-esteem. It may be getting you what you want, though, in a very circular way.

Often passive people appear so helpless that others may look after or protect them. Terrific! You can be taken care of and retain two great myths in your make-up:

- ✦ I'm not capable of or willing to make decisions.
- ✦ If I do not express my wants, needs or feelings, I can blame others when things do not go my way.

Yuck. If you have a pressing need to remain a child, be passive. You will never have a sense of power in your life, nor will you get what you want. This seems singularly self-defeating if it is your primary approach to your relationships.

Of course, there will times when you are not attached to the outcome of a decision. You don't care which movie you see. (Why are you going to the movies, then?) You don't care which ethnic restaurant you visit. (You may be too tired to make a decision and just want to eat *something*.) You understand when you are passed over for promotion for the third time. (I don't believe you.)

The Price Of Passivity

- ✦ You abdicate your opportunity to take control of your life, your career, your relationship, or your outcomes. (Doesn't that sound attractive?)

✦ You demonstrate a lack of respect for your own needs and rights. (Doormats are easily walked over . . . and you're laying down.)

✦ Your relationships are often not particularly satisfying. (Now there is an understatement.)

✦ Your ability to create intimacy will be compromised. (How can you be intimate with someone when you simply won't tell them what you like, want, need?)

✦ You fear the disapproval, anger, or disappointment of others. (Double-edged sword here: Err on the side of assertion. If they are going to disapprove, at least, give them your opinion to win their disapproval!)

✦ You actually annoy, irritate, and anger those around you with your lack of conviction and clarity. (This leads to them discounting you completely and then moving away or taking you for granted. Great alternatives, right?)

✦ People pity passive people. And then they become disgusted with them. (Great way to keep friends and significant others. First, you are their doormat. Then, they wear you out and throw you away.)

✦ Passive people often cannot control their emotions. They "stuff" their feelings, seldom saying what is so for themselves yet desperately wanting to be seen, known, and understood. This often leads to stress-related illnesses, absenteeism, and low productivity in the workplace. (The more passive you become, the more likely there will be someone willing, able, and ready to take advantage of you.)

✦ Passive people become resentful and turn that rage inwards. Then, beware. Their emotions are often expressed indirectly through sarcasm, criticism, withdrawal, or sabotage. Many a person who "went postal" was passive.

It is important to know the difference between a conscious choice to be passive because something is simply not important to you, and a default lifestyle when you think everyone is "doing it to you" because you let them!

AGGRESSIVE BEHAVIOR

Aggressive people are the easiest rhinos to identify. Are you working with one? Are YOU one? Aggressive people often seem to win in the short run. But, it's a "hit and run" kind of winning. They knock someone over and, while that person is down grab the goodies and escape leaving the poor victim dazed and amazed. It's annoying, to say the least.

One of the most annoying things about that kind of behavior is that these rhinos seem to be very good at protecting *themselves*. Who would ever think they are vulnerable? Think about this: a person who has such a great need to control others is likely afraid they would not be able to earn respect in worthwhile ways.

One of my executive coaching clients asked me to work with his office manager for a few sessions. When I asked why, he said,

> "She is very efficient and quite effective. She brought tremendous experience and expertise to my business. She knows what needs to be done and she is pro-active. I need her skills, however, my staff don't trust her, like her, or turn to her. In fact, they are afraid of her."

Great! Excellent! Good hiring choice! In one way, it was a good choice. The office manager did get things done and the owner could count on that. On the other hand, the office tension was thick and tempers were short. She was simply too aggressive.

As we worked together, her fears surfaced. People older or different from her made her feel unsafe and unsure. She thought they were judging her negatively. People who needed instruction and supervision were annoying and unworthy. She thought they were "lesser" beings who were not shouldering their workload. For every human condition, she had a defense. None of it, in her opinion, was a reflection of how she was behaving.

Happy ending. As we worked together, she began to change her perception, her perspective, and her behavior. She reframed her view and felt less threatened by others. In turn, she was then able to become more assertive and save her aggression for warding off bears from her campsite or stomping muggers to the ground.

The Price Of Aggression

- ⊕ You feel isolated, alienated, and feared. (Hmm, smells like a rhino.) No one wants to be around you for long because your unpredictability drains so much energy. If I don't know when you are going to blow, I lose energy being ready to protect myself from you. (Of course, if I am a very passive person, I can simply lie down and let you walk up and down my accommodating spine, creating a symbiotic relationship . . . like a rhinoceros and a tick bird!)

- ⊕ You may become ill . . . and so may the people around you. Keeping yourself in a turmoil by watching for inequities, weaknesses, or chinks in the armor is exhausting. Then, all that exercise you get from jumping to conclusions and leaping into the fray can do you in. (And, that's not to mention the road kill you are leaving in your wake.)

- ⊕ You fear loss of self-control yet you're always a moment away from it. Your aggression is aimed at keeping folks in line and at bay, yet your fear is always "what if they say no?" Habitual aggressors walk a very sharp edge fraught with danger on both sides. (Get help. See a counselor. Get a coach with a strong psychology background. Do something right away to prevent disaster . . . and a heart attack!)

- ⊕ You might set off another aggressor and the battle will be on. If you insist on running over other rhino's dung heaps, don't be surprised when you are attacked! (Oh, and rhinos are often inadvertently killed in these incidents. Beware.)

- ⊕ You internalize your guilt—if you have any sensitivity at all—and it hurts you. Then, you strengthen your arsenal and go back to git 'em. (You know where that cycle leads.)

- ⊕ Aggressive people dehumanize themselves. They have a tendency to love things, tasks, situations, and outcomes, and simply *use* people to achieve their own objectives. These are the worst of the worst in the aggressive category. (Hopefully, this is not you in any way.)

- ⊕ Aggressive people have to watch their backs . . . or think they do. Their heightened concern for their safety from force, violence, and retaliation can cause paranoia to set in. (And, just because you're paranoid doesn't mean they're not out to get you, right?)

ASSERTIVE BEHAVIOR

First and foremost, assertive behavior demonstrates that you:

- ✦ know who you are;
- ✦ know what you want;
- ✦ know how you want to be treated;
- ✦ have the communication skills to be effective;
- ✦ value yourself;
- ✦ stand up for your feelings, ideas, beliefs, and needs;
- ✦ take responsibility for meeting as many of your own needs as you can;
- ✦ work to equalize power in relationships;
- ✦ express your legitimate rights;
- ✦ respect others' legitimate rights to express their wants, needs, and feelings;
- ✦ seek open, honest relationships with others;
- ✦ choose your own behavior along with the consequences consciously.

Wow! Assertiveness has a lot going for it. I hope that just reading those characteristics makes you say, YES, I WANT THAT! Or, does it scare the liver right out of you? It takes courage to become a basically assertive person. You have to believe that you are worth it.

One of the most telling questions that I ask my clients is

"Are you worthy of tremendous success?"

What is your answer? If you do not believe you are worthy of tremendous success, you will sabotage yourself at every turn. And, if you happen to be particularly passive, you'll blame it on others, on your past, on your lack of opportunities, or worse, your luck. No escape. Your attitude comes from you. You decide.

The good news is that you can change your mind in a nanosecond!

Your inner dialogue is completely within your control. It may be an old—and negative—habit AND you can change it with practice and self-awareness. You may need help. Asking for help from a colleague, counselor or coach is not a weakness. It is definitely a strength. Asking for help when you need it demonstrates your willingness to move towards what you most want. How could that be anything but strong?

**Assertiveness increases trust and respect,
and strengthens relationships. Be assertive.**

**In a hierarchy every employee tends to
rise to his level of incompetence.**

Laurence J. Peter

ARE YOU A "VALUE-ADDED" EMPLOYEE?

What is your focus when you go to work? Are you thinking "What can I give today?" or "What can I get?" Both questions are important, however, the former will get you further, faster. It's that simple.

Often, when I am consulting with a company or team, the hew and cry is "The company/management does not do enough for me/us." This may certainly be true, however, my first question is the opposite, "What are you doing for the company/management?" That's the way the equation works best. You give and then you get. Strangely, that's the way it works best in any relationship. Have you noticed that?

What you pay attention to expands.[1] If you focus on what you think you are *not* getting, that overshadows everything. Attitudes shift and conversations turn into whining sessions. Soon, morale dips and everyone is complaining. Often, the complaints have grown completely out of proportion and no one remembers why they were attracted to the company in the first place.

You can change this. Be a "value-added" employee. Build your strengths rather than focusing on company weaknesses. What a concept! You choose your focus and attitude. You choose how you use your time. You choose your perceptions and perspectives. Use that power to become value-added!

I'm not talking about giving 'til it hurts. I'm talking about using your energy to focus on your career path. Sure, there are employers who devour employees and spit them out spent, burned out, and disillusioned. They exist. If you're working for one of those—and examine it carefully to be sure—move on.

I am talking about your choices to create the career you want.

- ✦ How do you want to be seen in the workplace?
- ✦ How does your current position support your progress towards your goals?
- ✦ Why did you choose this career?
- ✦ What is your plan and how can you best follow that blueprint in your present position?

BE PRO-ACTIVE IN YOUR OWN LIFE.

How do you want to be seen in the workplace? As competent, confident, and valuable, or as adequate, mediocre, and expendable? Unless you are working for Attila the Hun, the way folks see you is mostly in your control. Good employees come to work on time, do their tasks well, and cause few waves. Great employees do all that and more.

- ✦ They are focused on the company's mission and vision.
- ✦ They can be excellent team-players and excellent leaders when needed.
- ✦ They are clear about their own purposes and visions, and know why they have chosen to work where they work.
- ✦ They care about others and help them to achieve their goals.

✤ They do these things because it clearly moves them further along their career paths. It is in their own best interest to do so. They have their eyes on the prize.

Here are a few secrets:

Many folks would rather complain about things than fix them. By being a "fixer", you are being value-added.

Many folks would rather find fault than good. By catching people doing things well and commenting on it, you are being value-added.

Many folks would rather find out what they can get away with than what they can give. By giving just a little more than expected, you honor yourself and you are being value-added.

Many folks would rather feel "done wrong" than state their needs and boundaries. By clearly communicating what you need and want, you are saving time and energy . . . and being value-added.

Which side of these equations are you working from? Only one will get you where you want to go . . . although you'll have much more company on the other. Your choice!

1. Read Dr. Shaler's motivating book, *What You Pay Attention to Expands.* (San Diego:People Skills Press, 2003). Available at Amazon.com or at her website, www.OptimizeInstitute.com

**Example is not the main thing in
influencing others; it's the only thing.**

Albert Schweitzer

WHY CAN'T THEY BE MORE LIKE ME?

Do you think your workplace would benefit from being staffed by clones of yourself? Would that solve all the little issues that often annoy, irritate, or upset you? Really? Well, who would do the things you do not like to do? Who would make the coffee, empty the recycling, go to the post office?

Learning to value our differences is a major psychological hurdle to get over. It seems that no matter where you look, people are in conflict—even at war—because their beliefs are different, their roots are different, or their history is different. In the workplace, it may be because their approach, background, or style is different. The problem only occurs, of course, when either party makes an assumption: an assumption that being different means one side is important or right, and the other is secondary or wrong.

Sure, some differences are very troubling. If you are working or living with a person who hears voices telling them to hurt others, this is an unacceptable difference. It is clear that help is required. Most differences, however, are only as irritating as we decide to *let* them be. That's where your power lies.

Any way you look at it, we usually like people who are like ourselves. We are more comfortable with them and more accepting of their little quirks and slips. We tend to clan together with those who share our interests, world views, political attitudes, and general outlooks on life, don't we? That's natural. BUT, that does not make the other folks wrong!

In the workplace, there is real value in differences. This is particularly true when working on a project. Differing points of view, managed with excellent communication skills and a healthy respect for one another, often lead to greater creativity. Folks with different skills and interests can separate a project into reasonable parts and do an excellent job of the finished product. If the group were fully comprised of folks who thought alike, would there be such a likelihood of creativity?

Seek to understand the folks around you. Understanding one another is the important part. You may not be ready to value them, but do make the effort to understand where they look at the world from. Don't guess, though. Ask and listen.

The psychologist, Carl Jung, suggested that the notion of being understood really means "to be embraced, to be interpreted correctly."

- ✦ Do you take the time to understand the people who you feel are quite different from you?
- ✦ Do you demonstrate interest?
- ✦ Do you truly listen?
- ✦ Do you listen with an open mind and a willingness to understand?

It's a good idea to understand the people you're working with.
There is an excellent chance you will learn something valuable!

COMPETITION IS BEST KEPT TO YOURSELF!

A re you playing golf at work? Richard Behrens, Golf Grand Master, says,

"Good golf is all in the mind . . . the golfer's own lower mind, and how the person perceives the situations s/he finds . . . on the course are the major reasons s/he suffers from unsatisfactory play."[1]

> **Competition creates better products, alliances create better companies.**
>
> Brian Graham

It's all in the mental discipline of the game. This aspect of the process often eludes players. *The same principles that affect your golf shots apply to the workplace.*

+ Have you ever talked yourself out of executing a project that is well within your ability?

+ Have you carried anger with you from another poor situation and had it affect your entire day?

✦ Have you let that anger spill out inappropriately and damage a relationship?

In any game played with other people, there is a winner. Either an individual or a team wins. Just about everyone who enters a competition does so with the desire to win. This is healthy and natural, however, if you have a *need* to win, things change.

The need to win drives your mind into the future and away from the matters at hand. This is a problem. It is impossible to do something for pleasure and have a need to win. That *need* will eradicate the pleasure of simply doing the activity.

How is this applied in the workplace? Hopefully, you enjoy your work. (If not, you've already placed yourself in a difficult situation that requires careful reflection.) You want to be there. The tasks interest you. You enjoy the environment and the people—most of the time. Great start! This allows you to look forward to your work and your workplace.

Imagine if you went to work each day with the attitude,

> "I just have to find ways to show everyone that I am better than my peers."

Uh oh, trouble ahead. This is the *need* to win. Doing your work to the best of your ability because you enjoy it and you care about it demonstrates your *desire* to win. And, as in golf, you are competing with yourself.

✦ Do you have a desire to win?
✦ Can you do better quality work?
✦ Can you pay more attention to details?
✦ Can you bring the project in slightly ahead of schedule?
✦ Will you take time to be supportive to colleagues?
✦ Do you treat folks respectfully?
✦ Do you refrain from gossip and bad-mouthing?

✦ AND, can you do all that a little better than you did yesterday because you WANT to?

If you answered yes to every question, you have the *desire* to win. Your desire to do your best shows that you are truly on your own team. *That's where you want to be—on task and on target with your desire to demonstrate* *what you value and who you are.* You do that by living in integrity with what is important, significant, and valuable to you. Your attention is not on showing others up, but rather on bringing your best to the workplace.

Excellent golfers play to improve on yesterday's performance. Even when they are playing in tournaments, their focus is on doing their best, not on beating others. They keep the fun in their game, too.

The best keep their competition to themselves. There's much to be learned from the game of golf. How are you playing?

1. Richard Behrens, *Golf: The Winner's Way : Applying the Teachings of Martial Arts.* (St. Paul, MN: Llewellyn Publications, April 1, 1999)

I have yet to find the man, however
exalted his station, who did not do
better work and put forth greater
effort under a spirit of approval than
under a spirit of criticism.

Charles Schwab

CRITICISM OR FEEDBACK?
NO DIFFERENCE IF IT HURTS!

Just the word *criticism* can make our knees shake. No one likes being criticized . . . unless, of course, they have a very masochistic turn of mind: they actually get pleasure from being humiliated or mistreated. (But that's a whole other issue for another book.)

In business, we often have to offer criticism even if we carefully call it *feedback*. The dictionary makes a distinction: *feedback* is an expected part of a process, *criticism* is individually-based and tends to be quite subjective. Simply put, criticism is likely negative leaning towards judgmental, where feedback supposedly offers clear, shared guidelines that can be easily talked about. No matter what the dictionary says, we commonly feel no difference if either is offered without skill or sensitivity.

Any performance review opens the door for criticism. Two things are often true about performance reviews:

1. No one likes doing them

2. No one likes receiving them

. . . when good communication skills and good feedback skills are not operating.

THE BASICS WE NEED TO CONSIDER . . .

What can we do to offer criticism that can be:

a. heard

b. absorbed

c. understood

d. about the work and the workplace, not the person?

Now, that last one is tricky. Without an excellent—or even adequate—skill set, directing judgmental information to an employee in a negative, personal way does much damage. Criticism can be conveyed in light of corporate culture, team decisions, goal achievement or mission needs. (There is very seldom a reason to judge character and never a time to make inferences about poor genes, upbringing, brain power, or the like!)

It is difficult to "win friends and influence people" with criticism poorly delivered—blurted out, under duress, with no skills. Abraham Lincoln said:

"He has a right to criticism, who has a heart to help."

That eliminates those people who derive great pleasure from making others cringe from the pool of folks who offer feedback. Those people need skills, or, a good talking to by someone who understands the quote!

Recently, I worked with an executive coaching client. I was hired by HR to work with a VP. They described her this way:

> "She is curt, abrupt, abrasive with an unpleasant edge who we would really like to keep for her other skills. Can you help?"

That was their question. My question was:

> "Does this person know how you feel and have any compelling desire to change?"

They indicated she was willing to accept coaching. What a nightmare! The company did not want to tell her that she was on the edge of being fired. They didn't want to tell her that they hired me to give her the skills OR they were going to fire her. And, she would not return my emails or phone calls because she did not want to change . . . or, even, admit a need for change. These folks needed serious skill upgrades!

Why is feedback important?

That's a simple one. People like to know where they stand. Vagueness doesn't cut it. Want proof? There was a survey done not so long ago by Working Woman Magazine. The results might be surprising:

> "48% of respondents suffer from lack of feedback & 69% are looking for another job because of that lack."

Want a second opinion? Winston Churchill offers this:

> "Criticism may not be agreeable, but it s necessary. It fulfills the same function as pain in the human body. It calls attention to an unhealthy state of things."

Enough said!

Why do people resist giving others feedback?

- "If I put it off, the issue may go away."
- "If I put it off, someone else may do it."
- "I don't want to risk losing approval by telling him/her what I really think."
- "I know I don't have the skills to do it well and I don't want to blow it."
- "Maybe they'll get fired if I just wait."

Add your own reasons for resisting. Whether it is at work, at home, at church, or on the bowling team, no one really wants to hear criticism and we all know it. We also know that it is important, valuable, and constructive when done well.

PREPARATION IS KEY.

In Canada long ago, I was a Girl Guide. Their motto has stuck with me always, "Be Prepared". Whether you are about to go on a trip, ask for a date, negotiate a loan, or give feedback, preparation is key.

Communication about sensitive matters REQUIRES preparation. Yes, people have blurted out a marriage proposal and everything has gone well. It CAN happen, however, it is much wiser to plan. You want to think through:

- What are realistic expectations?
- What behaviors do I think are most important to discuss?
- Is this the right/best time for the feedback session?
- What outcome do I want?
- How can I best reach that outcome?
- What do I know about myself that I need to keep in check, or, bring to the forefront to make this the best session for both of us?
- What is going well?
- What is the most important thing that needs changing?

AND . . .

CAUTION #1: Do NOT give feedback when you are already in a bad mood, looking for a scapegoat, or simply wanting to get it over with before tomorrow. This is a relationship issue and, in most cases, you can choose optimum timing.

CAUTION #2: Be sure the issue is worthy of criticism, and not simply coming from frustration and upset on your part. It could be your pet peeve, yet not affect others in any detrimental way!

CAUTION #3: Do NOT compare people. Often tempting but just don't do it. All that does is revisit sibling rivalry issues. Work with each person's strengths and areas best improved. Comparison is a trap!

CAUTION #4: No "hit & run" feedback. No broad-siding. This is NOT an attack, it is a learning conversation. Do NOT give feedback if you do not have time for a conversation. Do NOT give negative criticism without some balancing positive feedback. (If the person has no redeeming qualities, it's time to part company, not give feedback.)

CAUTION #5: NO threats or ultimatums unless it truly is the end. Those are most likely to fall out of your mouth if you have not prepared adequately. They come from issues of control, dominance, or sheer frustration. Not so helpful in the workplace!

CAUTION #6: Feedback is NOT about blame. It's about generating improvement! Be sure you are focused on the right thing—what you want. It's too easy to harp on what you don't like, don't want or won't stand for. Do NOT fall into that trap.

OK, YOU'RE PREPARED. NOW, WHAT?

THE CONVERSATION . . .

- Open the conversation with brief pleasantries. *You both know why you're there.*

- Ask permission to offer constructive criticism. *What? You think they'll say no?*

- Give the other some weight in the conversation. *Yes, it's a conversation.*

- Ask for and listen to their thoughts, issues, reasons with an open mind. *That's why you scheduled enough time to make this productive, remember?*

- Use neutral language to describe behavior. *Resist, grasshopper, impute no motives!*

- Talk about desired behaviors most. *Ah, just when you thought you could let it all out.*

- Leave the word "you" out of the conversation unless you are praising. No blame. *We're going for improvement of the team, the system, the output, the profitability.*

- Be sure both of you understand what changes and why changes are in order before ending the meeting. *Yes, it may take more time than what makes you comfortable.*

- Limit the feedback to the top item or two. *Overwhelming them and leaving them for dead is not a constructive strategy.*

- Use open-ended questions to elicit thoughts and feelings. Those are questions you cannot answer with just "yes" or "no".

- Do NOT leave without a mutual understanding of:
  - What is next?
  - By whom?
  - By when?
  - Why?

- Create an encouraging, positive, forward-moving intention before leaving.

Golden rule of difficult conversations:
BE HARD ON ISSUES AND SOFT ON PEOPLE!

APPRECIATION IS NEVER WASTED

T*hank you.* So good to hear. So simple to say. So, why are so many folks longing to hear it?

There is little that goes further towards improving relationships than a genuine "Thank you." You know that. Why, then, do so many folks have difficulty with it?

Are we moving too quickly to notice what others do for us? Do we just expect so much that we fail to acknowledge the little things? Is there some small part of us that refuses to give what we're not getting?

> I consider my ability to arouse enthusiasm among men the greatest asset I possess. The way to develop the best that is in a man is by appreciation and encouragement.
>
> Charles Schwab

You have probably heard, "It's part of your/his/her job. It's your *responsibility*." Sure, it may be. Does that mean that it does not deserve acknowledgment? You can bet it would be acknowledged if it was *not* done! At home, we often take each other for granted. We *expect.* We say things like, "If you really loved me, you would _____." Those are expectations delivered in a bartering mode. Where is the appreciation for what they do? Do you expect that the garbage will go out or the dishes will be put away? Why? Because it's *their job*? How about saying thank you? Everyone likes recognition for the things they do. Giving it is a very easy habit to acquire.

Have you ever lived with teenagers? The easiest way to engage them is to catch them doing something right. That means saying thank you when they do it, too. If you think this is too easy, try it for a month. Tell them what you see that you like, what you like about what they are doing/wearing/thinking. Forget about adding anything about what you don't like. You'll see the relationship change positively. Still sound too easy? Try it!

Simply look and each day you'll find many things worthy of acknowledgment. Stop and appreciate what IS being done for you . . . and, say so. William James, the great American psychologist, said,

> "The deepest craving of the human nature is the need to feel appreciated."[1]

Is there a part of you that longs to be seen, recognized, and acknowledged? Every person feels better when they are appreciated. Let's not be too busy, or too important, to stop, see, and acknowledge the contributions of others. And, once is not enough. Each time the garbage is taken out or the report is handed in, each time they bring you coffee or extend themselves on your behalf, say thank you.

There is another side to appreciation. It is equally as important as recognition. William James calls it wisdom. He says,

> "The art of being wise is the art of knowing what to overlook."

That's worth thinking about, isn't it? Do you know what to overlook and when to overlook it? That can only happen when you step outside of yourself, your needs and wants, and see another person wholly. When you can calibrate what is most important at any given moment in a relationship, you are very wise .

Conflict is worst when folks do not know what to overlook. When tempers flare and approaches differ, nitpicking escalates. When deadlines loom and funding fails, fingers point. A wise person takes a step back and looks at the whole picture.

- ✦ What is happening here?
- ✦ What do we want to happen?
- ✦ What outcomes do we want this exchange to create?

This is the time to focus on appreciation and follow it with team problem-solving. The same is true in all relationships. If things are getting tense, reflect on the last time you felt appreciated. More importantly, when was the last time you found something to appreciate in someone else? This could well be at the bottom of the anger, frustration, fear, or hurt that you are feeling. You can fix this with good communication and assertion skills.

Start with yourself. Give first. Demanding to receive when the other person is feeling empty will only escalate the negatives. Whoever is most sane at the moment in any relationship is the one responsible for that relationship. Let that be you.

Appreciation is never wasted. Find things to acknowledge. Notice what others do well. Catch them doing things right. (There it is again!)

Notice what others do for you. Offer your thanks.
You'll feel better. And, very soon, it will come back to you.

1. William James. *The Varieties of Religious Experience.* (New York: Touchstone, 1997 [Simon & Schuster, 1997])

The illiterate of the 21st century will not be those who cannot read and write, but those who cannot learn, unlearn, and relearn.

Alvin Toffler

RHINO RANTS:

COMMUNICATION SKILLS
TO SAY WHAT YOU MEAN
AND BE HEARD

. . . leaders are people who are
able to express themselves fully . . .
they know who they are, what their
strengths and weaknesses are, and
how to fully deploy their strengths
and compensate for their weaknesses.
They also know what they want, why
they want it, and how to communicate
what they want to others, in order
to gain compensation and support.
Finally, they know how to achieve their
goals. The key to full self-expression
is understanding one's self and the
world, and the key to understanding
is learning–from one's own life and
experience.

Warren Bennis, "On Becoming a Leader"[1]

CAN WE TALK?

D o those words "Can we talk?" encourage you to communicate, or strike terror into your heart? For many folks, the latter is true. They have learned that the person's next words may be difficult to hear. It is common to expect confrontation to follow, and it can be intimidating.

It is so much easier to engage in communication than to truly communicate. What's the difference? *Communication* indicates information going out. Send out a press release. Leave voice-mail. Post a bulletin. Write a memo. *To communicate* requires information going in both directions. No problem with the first. Often, big problems with the second. (See page 38.)

What have you learned about communicating in the past? Have you had positive, warm, constructive discussions where difficulties could be spoken and heard? Discussions in which feelings were understood and accepted? Terrific! Then "Can we talk?" sounds like a marvelous opportunity to strengthen your relationship. If that has not been your experience, there are some guidelines that may be useful to you.

As George Bernard Shaw says,

> "The problem with communication is the illusion that it has been accomplished."

"Can we talk?" means someone wants to be heard. So, the first important thing is your willingness to listen. What's scary about listening? The other person probably wants you to change a behavior. That can cause you to feel insecure and defensive. If you behave from either of those two places, you know where that will lead. Either you'll cower and feel bad, or, you'll get angry and feel bad, or you'll leave and feel worse. Not much of a choice!

So, first decide to enter the conversation with equal willingness to speak *and* listen. Then, take the next step. Be willing to *respond* to what you hear, rather than *react*. Big difference. A great place to begin is to take a slow breath in through your nose and out slowly through your mouth and ask yourself,

> "What do I want as the result of this exchange?"

This increases your consciousness and helps you remain centered. Then, simply ask for more information. Here's a start,

> "Please tell me more."

Why would you do something as risky as asking for more? So that you are fully informed before you respond. Makes sense, doesn't it?

Now you have done another very good thing. You have demonstrated interest in the speaker. You have also followed the good advice of Steven Covey when he said,

> "Seek first to understand, then be understood."[2]

It buys you time and information. Very wise.

When you do speak, speak about yourself and your perceptions, feelings and desires. Make a conscious effort to remove the word *you* from the conversation at this point. Tell the other person what you see, feel, and hear. You can use a sentence like this,

> "When ___ happens, I feel ___. What would make that easier/ better/more productive would be if ___could happen."

Notice, no mention of the other person? Speak only of events. OK, OK, you want to say something like:

> "When you speak to me in that tone of voice, my skin crawls and I want to smack you."

Take a deep breath. Ask yourself once more what you want from this exchange. If the answer is to never see this person again in your life, then say it any way you like. It won't matter. If, perchance, you will see this person again and you truly want to improve the ability to communicate, one way to express your feelings would be:

> "When I hear a voice that sounds condescending (or like the one my father used when he was mad), I get very upset. I cannot hear what is being said because I am so affected by the tone of voice. In fact, it irritates me to the point of just wanting to lash out. I want this relationship to work (or improve) and I want to be able to listen."

Now, if this is a totally new way for you to express yourself, that other person may be in shock for a moment or two. In fact, it may take them a while to believe your new approach is honest. Just keep doing it. It will become second nature to you and others will begin to respond very positively. Sure, in the beginning, it may feel very awkward and, even, silly. You may feel that you should just be able to be accepted the way you are with no need to change. You're right, of course, if you want to risk the other person avoiding you or going away altogether.

These guidelines are only for those who value their relationships and want to give them the best chance to be both respectful and improving. Learn to communicate!

1. Warren G. Bennis. *On Becoming A Leader.* (New York: Perseus Books, 1994.)
2.. Steven Covey. *The Seven Habits of Highly Effective People.* (New York: Fireside, 1990)

If all my talents and powers were
to be taken from me by some
inscrutable Providence, and I had my
choice of keeping but one, I would
unhesitatingly ask to be allowed
to keep the Power of Speaking, for
through it, I would quickly recover all
the rest.

Daniel Webster

SPEAK UP!

Ever been in a meeting and had something important to say . . . and remained silent? You may have felt the flush of the good idea and the rising adrenalin. You may have moved to the front of your seat and readied your body to speak . . . and then didn't. What stopped you?

Certainly, there is wisdom in knowing when to speak and when not to. Knowing the politics of a situation or the time constraints, you may choose not to speak. Often though, you may have a unique view, perspective, issue, or concern that needs to be raised. That contribution would add a new dimension to the discussion or change the decision about to be made. You may feel strongly about a new policy and your silence allows folks to think you agree. Is that the message you wish to send?

Recently, I was involved in the creation of a new management team for a department in a public sector organization. This brought together four people who previously felt they were in a pecking order and changed them into a cohesive decision-making team. Two of the four had strong opinions which they were very comfortable expressing. Two were very quiet. In forming the team, we discussed this dynamic. How were they each going to best contribute to the team? We talked about the possibility that the talkative two could overpower the silent two. In fact, they might even do the talking for them! Focusing on the fact that each person was hired because of his or her expertise in a distinct field, it was soon decided that each person's opinion was vital to good decision-making.

The two who were quiet were definitely as competent as the others. Increasing their level of comfort with adding their voices to the group was important. Two things were agreed upon:

- ✦ each person would speak on every issue, and
- ✦ each person would take responsibility for doing so.

One of the natural "talkers" offered to ask the quiet two for their opinions. This seems like a good idea on the surface, however, as a rule, it is a poor idea.

Why is it a poor idea? Simple. If one person takes responsibility for the contributions of others, there are two new kinds of control being encouraged: the talker has control over when the others are asked for their opinions; and the silent could be waiting to be asked, making their contribution the talker's responsibility. Neither of these options are optimal.

Each person must understand that he or she was hired to contribute their expertise and experience to the team. It is the responsibility of the individual to contribute. For the talkers, that was easy. In fact, it was enjoyable. For the quiet folks, two things seemed to be true: one of them only felt it necessary to contribute if she disagreed with the direction of the conversation, and the other was very shy. What to do?

With some individual coaching, each team member began to monitor involvement in the meetings. Those for whom it was difficult undertook to, at least, say when they agreed or disagreed. Those for whom it was easy undertook to leave some airtime free. Often, it is a challenge to find a quiet moment to summon up the gumption to speak!

When you have something you feel is important to contribute to a meeting, formulate your thoughts, take a deep breath and jump in. **It's unlikely anything life-threatening will happen.** It's a little like learning to swim. The first few times you may get a mouthful of water and sputter a little. You may find yourself gasping for air. You may flail around a little, but with practice things even out and you make progress. Yes, it may feel awkward. Yes, you may discount the importance of what you have to say before you say it. But jump in. You are there to offer your skills and learning. It is your responsibility.

Some tips for handling those who only value the sound of their own voices:

- ⊕ **Wait, Prepare, Be Ready!** They have to take a breath sometime. Be ready to step in and take that opportunity.

- ⊕ **Agree With Them.** Begin with "I agree, (name), with part of your opinion . . . " and go on to offer your thoughts. Being agreed with, even in part, will encourage them to listen to you.

- ⊕ **Use Positive Language.** Tell folks what you think would be best and why, rather than telling them what is wrong with their ideas. Again, you may capture their attention.

- ⊕ **Have Confidence In Your Ideas.** Clarify your thoughts prior to the meeting. You may even want to make some notes. Being prepared will make it more likely that you will have some energy behind your points of view and, therefore, be more likely to express them.

- ⊕ **Be Brief And Specific.** This is a great tip for everyone at the meeting. Stay on the topic and the point. Give your thoughts and reasons in short sentences, then stop and let others respond. This is the way business gets done! Who wants interminable meetings?

Speak up! You have the right and responsibility to do so. That is why you have the job!

**In interpersonal communication, there
must be an ongoing and perceived
consistency between what you say
and how you say it.**

Janet G. Elsea

SAY WHAT YOU MEAN

We have great expressions for not saying what we mean. We are beating around the bush. She tells little white lies. He's hedging. They are waffling. What causes us to shy away from saying what we mean? From telling the truth even when it's tough? *Lack of confidence, clarity and competence.*

The easiest thing to do is to **acquire the competence**. Communication skills are learned early, as are conflict management skills. We start picking these up long before we have language, by watching our families. We pick up tone of voice; we notice how sounds and facial expressions go together; then, we add body posture. Even babies know who to trust. They add up the face, body and voice and conclude whether you're OK or not.

Not much changes as we age. We still have those skills except that we start second-guessing ourselves and sometimes fail to pay attention to what our senses tell us. We start believing *what* we want to believe rather than *listening to the message* on all levels. If we listened, we would not buy things from people who make the hair on the back of our necks stand up. You would not believe that he really loves you when he regularly abuses you. You would believe the message of your senses rather than talk yourself into believing what you want to believe.

It's all about trust. When I am teaching my *How to Make an Entrance & Work a Room* program, I talk about what happens in the networking situation when you meet new people. This is no time for posturing and pretending. This is a time for sending a congruent message.

BE WHO YOU ARE!

Why do I make this point so strongly? We know that you never get a second chance to make a first impression. In a first meeting, you want to be yourself. Of course, put your best foot forward but make sure that you can back it up with all the other steps you are likely to take with that foot for a long time. Nothing is more disappointing than meeting someone you believe you want to do business with, or date, and finding, on the second meeting, they have morphed into someone else. Someone that causes you to wonder *What was I thinking?* Be who you are. Be congruent. Be sure your tone of voice, facial expression, body posture, words and actions match—all the time. That makes you trustworthy.

Clarity is essential. You have to know what you want to say. That means you have to know what you think and feel. This requires *honesty with yourself.*

In my experience as a speaker, therapist, and coach, I've learned most folks do not spend enough time with themselves to find out who they really are. In fact, many people will do anything to *avoid* spending time with themselves. Their time is filled with activity, leaving little time for reflection. Or, they want to gather everyone else's opinion and forget to trust their own.

What do you need to say? It may not be the most popular thing, or just what the other wants to hear. But, it may NEED to be said to keep your relationship on an honest basis.

You may be wondering, "What about saying something that will get me what I want?" Good question. Saying what you think the other person needs to hear, to get you what you want, is a great short-term solution. If you are never going to see the person again, you may get away with it. If you are going to see them or work with them regularly, you have just undermined trust.

Have you ever been duped, persuaded, or bullied into buying something you did not want? Are you anxious to see that salesperson again? Enough said. Are you honest with yourself? When that small voice inside says something's not right with this conversation or person, are you listening? I hope so. You pick up on clarity and congruence with much more than your ears. Listen with all your senses.

When you are speaking, you KNOW when you are telling the truth. It rings and resonates. And, you don't have to remember what you said. The hardest part about lying is that you have to remember what you said and live with the consequences! You've likely had the experience of dragging out a situation well past its due date. The longer you drag it out, the worse things get. We live in a world where people cover the truth to supposedly "spare the feelings" of the listener. This is nonsense! They simply don't want to say what they mean! They have not learned nor practiced the skills of honest communication. They are not competent, clear or confident in their own truth nor comfortable with the delivery. Do we all want to be living in denial all the time? Things need to be said, and often, the sooner the better.

When you are clear and competent, you will be confident. There will be nothing between you and the other person—no hedging, no hesitancy, no lies, no uncertainty. You will tell the truth with skill. You will have learned ways to phrase things that keep the accuracy of your facts and feelings and deliver them in ways that consider and protect the feelings of others. It's all in the skills . . . and they take practice.

Learn the communication skills to express yourself authentically. Take some classes. Ask for feedback from people you trust. In my teleseminars[1], I have many classes that will help you examine your communication and learn new skills and strategies . . . right on the telephone. So, it's easy to get the training. There's no excuse.

Life gets much simpler when you say what you mean and tell the tough truth. Get on it!

---

1. For the convenience of learning from the nearest telephone, visit www.OptimizeInstitute.com and click on Teleseminars. Your entire team can learn together, or, you can get the specific skills you need right away.

It is such a relief to be told the truth.

Katherine Anne Porter

TELLING THE TOUGH TRUTH

You have, no doubt, experienced either *having* to tell the tough truth, or *wanting* to tell the tough truth; and you've likely been *told* the tough truth once or twice too. Two things are true about these experiences. The truth is not always easy to tell, and it is not often easy to hear!

So what can you do to make both those things easier?

BE PREPARED

When you know that you are heading into a situation that could be touchy or difficult, where emotions may run high, or where harm could be done if care was not taken, prepare yourself. Be clear about your issues and concerns, and about your boundaries. If you have completely thought through your reasons, reactions, and responses to the situation, you will be far better prepared to express yourself clearly.

BE ASSERTIVE RATHER THAN AGGRESSIVE

Assertive statements contain no blame and no attack. Conveying both information and feelings objectively is respectful. Remember, when you are speaking about *your* feelings, you need to own them. Do not suggest that someone else creates those feelings for you . . . they are your particular reaction to your perceptions. When you need to tell the tough truth, take the time to express yourself fully. Give *your* perspective on the situation, *your* feelings about the situation, and *your* wants regarding the outcome or progress of the situation.

Here is an example:

> "I get very concerned when deadlines are approaching and I feel that the team is not pulling together well. It is my responsibility to bring this project in on time and it is important to me to do to this. This requires everyone being focused and collaborative."

This example demonstrates communication skills that lead to problem-solving dialogue.

BE SPECIFIC ABOUT WHAT YOU WANT TO HAPPEN OR HOW YOU WANT TO BE TREATED.

Whether in a work, family or social relationship, it is important that you take responsibility for teaching people how to treat you. If you do not tell someone how their behavior affects you, and it affects you negatively, then you are silently telling them that it is all right with you.

Done assertively, not aggressively, most people will listen and respect your boundaries. If they do not or will not, that is important information for you. You may choose to remove yourself from the relationship. Also, when someone treats you well, be sure to tell him or her how much you appreciate it. Catching folks doing things right is the best teaching tool of all!

Telling the truth is sometimes difficult, however, living with frustration, dishonesty, or anxiety is more difficult. Learning to tell the truth respectfully promotes good relationships.

John Powell wrote that "The genius of good communication is to be totally kind and totally honest at the same time."[1]

Practice can create that genius!

1. John Powell. *The Secret of Staying In Love: Loving Relationships Through Communication.* (Allen, TX: Argus Communications, 1974)

**Men occasionally stumble over
the truth, but most of them pick
themselves up and hurry off as if
nothing had happened.**

Winston Churchill

RHINO REALITY:
IIIIIIIIIIIIIIIIIIIIIIIIIIIIIIIIIIIIIIIIII

RHINOS, EVEN WHEN COURTING, SNORT AND SPAR WITH THEIR HORNS.

RULES FOR RECOGNIZING RHINOS:
IIIIIIIIIIIIIIIIIIIIIIIIIIIIIIIIIIIIIIIIIIIIIIIIIIIIIIIIIIIIIIIIIIIIIIIIIIIIIIIIIIIIII

RHINOS ARE MISSING VITAL, APPROPRIATE COMMUNICATION SKILLS.

**It is easy to fly into a passion—
anybody can do that—but to be angry
with the right person to the right
extent and at the right time and with
the right object and in the right way—
that is not easy, and it's not everyone
who can do it.**

Aristotle
ııııııııııııııııı

WANT TO GRAB THEM BY THE THROAT AND KNOCK THEM SENSELESS?

S ometimes you just do, don't you?

"Say that one more time and I'll send you to the moon."

"Miss another meeting and you're dead meat!"

"You may think that's cute. I think it's childish. Grow up."

You may not say these things, but they do run through the mind. They are the kinds of things that get your shoulders up around your earlobes by the end of the workday and send you scurrying for an over-priced coffee drink just to keep going. There are other solutions.

First, we need some practical things to simply do for ourselves on these occasions—without saying anything to the other person. You may think this is next to impossible, but try it!

⁣‖‖

I once married a man who was a calm, delightful man . . . bright, warm, caring. Soon after the wedding, I learned his big secret. He snored in that bring-the-house-down-and-calm-the-neighborhood-cats fashion. Really, the walls shook three rooms away. What to do? One solution would have been to have the marriage annulled, another to move to separate houses. Neither was an option, so, I learned something. I could take my attention away from his snoring and not be bothered by it. Do you think that was easy? It was easier than it sounds. (If you need some help with that concept, take a look at my book "What You Pay Attention to Expands".)

If he had been hurting anyone or impeding progress or was incompetent, another solution might have been the first to try. However, he was simply snoring loudly. With not too much effort, I found that turning my attention to thoughts of vacations, goals, love, or fantasy, and away from the rattling windowpanes, I no longer heard the snoring. It did take some practice. And, it worked. Sometimes, we just let people bother us too much and we take no responsibility for our own thoughts and attitudes. It is often easier to blame than to look within for answers.

Are you focusing on a co-worker's issues when you could be looking at your own? We humans like to look outside of ourselves for reasons when we are unhappy. We want SOMEONE to blame. It couldn't possibly be us! The most effective thought is to look within first.

"Is there something I am doing that is setting this person off?"

You know how to push someone's buttons, don't you? Many folks master this very early in life and they just keep practicing. What's in it for you? You can always make someone wrong and things seldom change. Therefore, you always have something to moan or whine about. Therefore, you can always be miserable . . . and you are choosing it. This is sheer lunacy!

"Am I communicating clearly?"

We've been carefully taught to be nice. Often that means that we do not communicate clearly. We are subtle, indirect or silent. Nothing will change if you cannot communicate well. If you happen to be a truly passive person, you may be hoping someone else will handle difficult people. Meanwhile, you are creating an ulcer. You must learn to be assertive. We all need to learn to be assertive, but, not aggressive.

"Am I teaching people how to treat me?"

If someone speaks to me in a way I find offensive, and I don't say anything, I've just told them it is all right with me. Sure, the first time, you may want to give someone the benefit of the doubt. Maybe they are having a bad day. The second time, though, speak up. It is not necessary to get really fancy with the words. Simple is good.

For example,

> "When I hear racist jokes, I feel very uncomfortable because, even though they can be humorous, they are at someone's expense. What would work for me is that we agree that you'll warn me before you tell one so that I can move away, or, you resist the urge to tell them around me. Would you agree to that? I would really appreciate it." (This is one of my pet peeves, so, I take care of it right away!)

Isn't that a better solution than squirming, judging or silently sending daggers in their direction? Taking care of business like this is empowering. You'll notice in the example above that I did not make the other person wrong. I spoke about my feelings and what would work for me. Then, I asked for agreement. I took care of business.

So, next time you want to whack someone upside the head, take a deep breath and use one of these strategies.

It's a jungle out there sometimes. Be prepared.

The right to be heard does not automatically include the right to be taken seriously.

Hubert Humphrey

ARE YOU BEING HEARD?

D o you stop and pay attention when someone speaks to you? Do you look at the speaker? Are you fully present? This is the most efficient and effective use of your time. How so? It is far less likely that you will misunderstand or have to ask for information to be repeated if you turn your attention to the speaker from the beginning.

The greatest compliment we can pay to another person is to truly listen to what they have to say.

You've experienced the non-committal grunts, "Uh-huh's" and "Oh, really's?" that indicate a person is hearing us but not listening to a word we are saying. *There is a very big difference between hearing and listening.* One uses only the ears, the other engages both the mind and the ears. When real listening occurs, the heart also participates!

Do folks truly listen when you speak? There are ways to increase the likelihood that your messages are being received. When you have something important to communicate or ask, take the time to prepare. Ask yourself,

"What do I want the outcome of this conversation to be?"

Work backwards from there.

When you are speaking, you want to be listened to. Otherwise, what would be the purpose of speaking? The same is true for everyone else.

WHAT TO DO TO GET THE ATTENTION OF OTHERS:

✤ **Use the name of person to whom you are speaking.** Everyone likes to hear his or her name, and it gives them a moment to turn their attention to you . . . and *return* their attention to you.

✤ **Check your timing.** If you wish to speak to someone about something that is very important, ask if this is a good time to talk. If it is not, set an appointment to talk at a specific time in the near future. There is no point in trying to talk to someone who is preoccupied, or whose priorities may be overriding your message at that moment.

✤ **Know what you want to say before you begin.** It shows respect for the listener—and for yourself—to have gathered your thoughts and prepared your approach before you initiate an important conversation.

✤ **Pay attention!** If people are obviously not listening, do not continue to talk. The pregnant pause becomes very obvious to them and encourages them to refocus on your message. *Stop talking until the receiver becomes aware of the silence.*

✤ **Eliminate distractions.** When you want to focus another's attention, shift your position to eliminate any distractions he or she might see behind you, or move closer to them in a non-menacing fashion to achieve more "communication closeness."

✤ **Capture attention.** If your listener's eyes are wandering, use a gesture to return their attention to you. Lift your upwardly-pointed index finger into their line of sight to make a point. Once they are focused on your movement and your finger, slowly bring it back to just under your chin. This will cause them to refocus on you and your words.

✛ **Delegate note-taking.** In a meeting, ask others to take notes. Just simply say,

"Do me a favor and take a couple of quick notes about this because it is important."

You'll be surprised when people just automatically pick up their pens and begin to write.

Remember, the responsibility for communication rests with you. Just because you said something does not mean anyone was *listening*, though it may appear that you were *heard*. Your message is important to your relationships. Use these tips to increase your effectiveness.

Don't just be heard. Be listened to!

**You can only get a true reaction,
response or understanding from
people when you speak
their own language.**

E. Pringle

IF YOU WANT THEM TO HEAR YOU, SPEAK THEIR LANGUAGE!

You've probably noticed that there are some problems with our communication system. We have to use words, which are often imprecise, awkward, and unable to capture the essence of what we want to say.

Problem #1

Words mean different things to different people. Even when we find what we consider to be adequate words, the listener may hear something else.

Problem #2

It is difficult to capture feelings in words. And, equally difficult to remove feelings from words. What a conundrum!

Problem #3

Listeners may not be listening. There's a big difference between listening and hearing: only the former engages the mind. Many folks begin formulating their response long before you've finished speaking. Trouble ahead!

Problem #4

The listener's prior experiences color your words for them. You are not alone. They are hearing every person who has ever spoken to them in your way or with your words, as you speak. Therefore, they decide where to place their attention and what their focus will be.

And we wonder why communication is difficult? It's enough to make you close your mouth forever!

Now, aside from those four problems, there are other considerations. Here are **some simple and significant ways to increase your chances of being accurately heard** and, hopefully, listened to.

1. **Know what is important to your listener.** Are they more interested in facts or feelings? Demonstrate your desire to communicate with them by starting with what is of greater interest to them.

2. **Know if your listener is more interested in the details or the decision.** Some folks are more comfortable with assessing and planning solutions than with making decisions and implementing them. Who are you speaking to? It is difficult to get a "decide-and-do" attitude from an "assess-and-solve" person. Similarly, it is more difficult to engage an "assessor" in a decision-making conversation. They will usually want to keep perfecting their plan. Acknowledge this and affirm their skill before asking them to decide.

3. **Know if your listener is results- or relationship-oriented.** Spending any time at all with small talk may drive a results-oriented listener to distraction. Conversely, offering no small talk can push away a relationship-oriented person. Lead with their interest and then you can present your point, or your point-of-view.

4. **Know the best timing for the conversation you wish to have.** If it could be in any way confrontational, be careful. Taking just five minutes to assess a situation prior to bringing up an issue can be very informative. Listen. Pick up the climate around your proposed listener. As with the philosophy of "pick your battles," so, is it wise to pick your times to increase the probability of being listened to.

5. **Know what you want to say.** Wading into a difficult conversation without clarity can quickly leave you drowning in misunderstanding. Think about the outcome you wish to create before you open your mouth. This will help you temper and tailor your approach to reach your desired goal.

A quick way to measure the appropriateness of your communication is to ask yourself,

"Am I willing to be spoken to in the way I am about to speak?"

If the answer is yes, proceed with assurance. If the answer is no, be very thankful you took that minute to think.

Communication can be tricky, but most tricks can be mastered.

I think the one lesson I have learned is that there is no substitute for paying attention.

Diane Sawyer

WHAT ARE YOU LISTENING FOR?

There are two sides to every conversation. Not only yours and theirs as you might think, but also the speaking and the listening. Too often, our main interest is in the speaking—OUR OWN!

You don't learn much when your mouth is open.

> **A good listener is not only popular everywhere, but after a while he knows something.**
>
> Wilson Mizner

Twenty years ago, *active listening* was a buzz phrase.
Those who took it to heart improved their relationships. Those who did not accept it made jokes about it. It's that simple.

It was then that the famous words were said:

> "I know that you believe you understand what you think I said, but I'm not sure you realize that what you heard is not what I meant."[1]

That's what comes from poor listening skills. As I've said before, there is a big difference between hearing and listening.

HOW DO YOU LISTEN?

- **Through A Filter Of Defense?** Are you always expecting and listening for blame, a problem, an inadequacy? If so, then you're listening from fear. Before the other person's mouth is open, you're expecting to have to defend yourself. *This is a communication killer!*

- **Like A Surgeon With Scalpel In Hand?** Do you cleanly separate the content—the words—from what those words might mean to the speaker? That keeps you from picking up the intent of the message. You also might believe that it keeps you safe from having to respond to that intent. Have you had the experience of someone parroting back your exact words with a completely different tone of voice, posture, inflection, or emphasis? Many folks use this, too, as a defense mechanism. It shows that you are not listening, but hearing what you perceive to be the truth.

- **With Your Heart Open?** Do you listen compassionately without judgment, with no intention of changing anything? When you listen this way, the speaker can speak—or even vent—safely because you are not jumping in with your point of view. You are not taking the words personally, have no reason to defend yourself, and can be completely free to listen to what is being said. *This is a big step up!*

- **With Full Attention To Purpose?** Do you give your full attention to the words, the inflection, the posture, the tone of voice, the facial expressions, the timing? Do you take in as much as you can to understand why the person is delivering this particular message at this particular time . . . to you, particularly?

You capture the essential reason the person is talking. There is no *you* in the equation! You don't jump to conclusions. You don't formulate your response while the other is still talking. You listen well so you can offer a response that is connected with the underlying reason the person has chosen to talk to you. *You are rare.*

✦ **With A True Interest In Finding Common Ground?** Are you listening for things you agree with, places where your values, ideas, desires, and goals and the speaker's intersect? What a concept! *This is truly enlightened listening.*

I was talking with a coaching client about just this subject. To make my point, I told him this story:

> When I was a teen, I studied piano and was well on my way to a career in music. In my parents' quest to make me the best, I was sent sixty miles away each week to study with a woman who was absolutely demanding. My fingers often ached from being hit with an ink stick pen.
>
> Although I chose a different career, one invaluable thing remains with me from this excellent, if brutal, teacher. I often entered sight-reading contests. That is where you are given a previously unseen piece of music and are expected to play it to the best of your ability one minute later for an audience. A situation fraught with tension. It's the moment where skills, ability, talent, and sheer good luck meet!
>
> Miss Tebo said this, *"Once you start to play, keep making beautiful music and let the bad notes fall on the floor."* These few words have impacted every part of my life!

So, in your communication, keep looking for the good, for the things you agree with, for the highest intent of the speaker. Keep those as your focus. Look for ways that your thinking intersects with that of the speaker. Be attuned to what you have in common. Listen for what the speaker is committed to rather than what he or she does not like. It's more efficient. You move forward together more effectively.

**Let the bad notes fall on the floor and keep the melody moving on.
You'll make much more beautiful music!**

1. Robert McCloskey, U.S. State Department spokesman, at a press briefing during the Vietnam War

**Take advantage of every opportunity
to practice your communication skills
so that when important occasions
arise, you will have the gift, the style,
the sharpness, the clarity and the
emotions to affect other people.**

E. James Rohn

NEWS FLASH! MEN & WOMEN COMMUNICATE DIFFERENTLY

There used to be a common myth that men did not respect women at work unless they behaved like men. Some women bought it and succeeded. Others accepted it and retreated. The truth is, though, that it is simply not true!

Men and women *do* communicate differently. Wise people—those who choose respect, trust, integrity, honesty, kindness—take the time to understand the differences. Those wise people are also the most likely to succeed. As both men and women learn to understand and interpret each other more accurately, they learn to respect one another, broaden perspectives, and gain valuable insights into being more productive. This is the foundation of *trust*.

The differences between men and women show up dramatically in communication. The words used may be the same, however, the meanings can be vastly different. We consistently misinterpret one another and, over time, we develop patterns that limit our perspectives . . . and our success. We can change these habits of perception.

Simple, easily definable differences are found in our non-verbal communication. Think of these:

- ✦ men require more space
- ✦ women establish more eye contact
- ✦ men use more gestures
- ✦ women smile more
- ✦ men touch more
- ✦ women speak more softly[1]

These are basic differences that innately affect our interactions!

Men and women differ greatly in their comfort with self-disclosure. Likely, self-disclosure differences are based on the cultural norms that guide the behavior of men and women. People in the United States tend to express their thoughts and feelings more openly than people in other cultures. In Japan, for example, self-disclosure is not seen as a primary means of developing relationships. The Japanese maintain relative privacy in their personal affairs. Eastern European cultures tend to conceal their thoughts and feelings in order to maintain harmonious relationships.

Women are more likely to self-disclose than men, research tells us. This is not a surprise, although it may be an overgeneralization of actual communication patterns. One sex may not actually disclose more than the other. It may be true that the two sexes have different reasons for disclosing: women disclose because they *like* the person, men because they *trust* the person. This would create a difference in the timelines for developing relationships . . . and an important consideration when building workplace relationships!

One of the major communication differences between men and women is their orientation. Men are more results-oriented while women are more relationship-oriented. You've likely read about this in John Gray's work on Mars and Venus. He says

"On Mars they use communication primarily to solve
problems and get a task done, while on Venus they use
communication for other purposes as well. For men,
communication in the workplace is primarily a way to
convey content or information. But for women it is much
more. Communication on Venus is a way to solve problems,
but it is also used to minimize stress and feel better, create
emotional bonds to strengthen relationships, and as a means
to stimulate creativity and discover new ideas". [2]

Big difference. Imagine the potential for misunderstanding and
misinterpretation! It's a double-edged sword. When women understand the
impact of this statement, they can more clearly see how they may be losing
the respect of the men at work. Conversely, as men understand it, they can see
how they may be losing the trust of the women.

Women often weaken their opinions by adding tag questions.

"Those were really solid points he made, weren't they?"

By adding the "weren't they?" it conveys the need to have their opinion
verified by the person to whom they are speaking. It infers uncertainty. They
seem to be looking for affirmation and agreement to validate their point of
view. It is a much stronger, clearer communication when left at:

"Those were really solid points he made."

Women also tend to use more intensifiers or modifiers, and hedges, than
men. This not only makes their communication wordier, it can again weaken
their transmission.

"This is SO important."
"That was QUITE lovely."
"It was SOMEWHAT interesting that . . ."
"It MAY be significant that . . ."

In many cases, words intended to intensify the communication actually
detract from it when speaking with men. Better to keep the communication
more direct, without the hedging in the passive voice.

"I think it is interesting that . . ."
"It is significant that . . ."

Of course, the flip side of these two ideas is also true. Men would find workplace communication more productive if they did solicit affirmation, agreement, and validation more often from their female counterparts. Their direct speech intended to convey certainty and conviction is often interpreted as being immovable simply because their thoughts or opinions are stated as facts. This reduces the likelihood of dialogue and the sharing of ideas and insights that could enhance the decisions being made.

Men tend to regard talk as a way to exert control, preserve independence, and enhance status. Women see talk as a way to establish and maintain relationships. Men and boys are more likely to describe others in terms of their abilities, whereas women and girls are more likely to describe others in terms of their self-concepts.

> Man: *"She writes well."*
> Woman: *"She thinks she's a good writer."*

Women are more likely to notice and describe others in terms of the interpersonal interactions, whereas men are more likely to note characteristics that are not related to social activities.

> Woman: *"He was just so easy to get along with."*
> Man: *"She likes football. Isn't that great?"*

These and so many other small but glaringly important differences affect the workplace. It is not that women want men to be more like them or vice versa. It is that when we wake up and realize we can do a much better job of communicating, by considering our acculturated differences, *we increase our likelihood of being understood, valued, respected, and trusted.*

**Take the time to learn to communicate effectively.
It's a skill. Learn it!**

1. Judy C.Pearson. *Gender and Communication.* (Dubuque, IA: Wm. C. Brown, 2nd ed. 1991)
2. John Gray. *Mars and Venus in the Workplace.* (New York: Harper/Collins. 2002.)

RHINO REALITY:
||||||||||||||||||||||||||||||||||||||||||||||

BOTH MALE AND FEMALE RHINOS
HAVE HORNS.

RULES FOR RECOGNIZING RHINOS:
|||||||||||||||||||||||||||||||||||||||||||||||||||||||||||||||||||||||||||||||||||

RHINO TRAITS ARE JUST THE SAME IN MEN
AS IN WOMEN: TERRITORIAL, SHORT-SIGHTED,
EXPLOSIVE, AND FEARFUL.

If any man wishes to write in a clear style, let him first be clear in his thoughts.

Johann Wolfgang von Goethe

PUT IT IN WRITING!

E ver been asked to "put it in writing"? Sure, you have. Did you immediately go to your desk and effortlessly record your thoughts and suggestions? Or, perhaps, you struggled and anguished?

For most people, producing useful, credible, and appropriate written communication requires careful thought. A wise practice. Putting it in writing is an excellent opportunity to showcase your communication skills. Writing something down not only clarifies an issue, it tends to gives the idea longevity, and, sometimes, a life of its own. Write carefully!

Written communication can be a double-edged sword. Done well, it can positively influence your career. Done poorly, quickly or thoughtlessly it can work against you. In a way, it IS written in stone. There it sits for everyone to see . . . and revisit.

CAUTION: **Avoid putting negative information in writing!**

Absolutely do not put negative information in writing unless it is accurately supported by verifiable fact. If writing about a person, state the facts in the passive voice and avoid the use of the word "you". For example,

"The work was completed well past the deadline."

rather than,

"You demonstrated no concern for our timelines."

One is a fact, the other, an assumption.

If you want or need to convey your opinion or perception, do so orally. Say it, rather than write it. There is a tendency for things to be scrutinized much more closely when they are in writing. Folks look for inaccuracies and "fodder for blame" in written communication. Written words scribed in the heat of the moment can sit in someone's files and become inadvertent weapons for years to come. A negative written communication can become a time bomb just waiting for the wrong person to detonate it. In *Getting Promoted*[1], Harry E. Chambers says,

"Enemies created in writing tend to have long life spans."

Be careful.

There are a few basic guidelines to keep in mind before you put pen to paper or allow your fingers to touch those keys. Sure, the important thing is the message itself, however, how that message is conveyed is a message in itself! Grammar counts. Poor grammar detracts from the message. You do not want anything to get in the way of your important message, do you? Your computer may be a help as it suggests grammatical changes, but, it is not infallible. You need the skills to catch errors. You know that your spell checker is limited otherwise it would not have left this poem intact:

Eye halve a spelling chequer
It came with my pea sea.
It plainly marcs four my revue
Miss steaks eye kin Knot Sea.
Eye strikes a key
And type a word
And weight four it two say
Weather eye am wrong oar write

It shows me strait a weigh.
As soon as a mist ache is maid
It nose bee fore two long
And eye can put the error rite
Its rare lea ever wrong.
Eye has run this poem threw it
I am shore your pleased two no
Its letter perfect awl the weigh
My checker tolled me sew.[2]

Make your writing concise. No one has the time or desire to read a novel about your topic. "Just the facts, Ma'am." That's what's needed.

Quality, not quantity, is best. Winston Churchill is reported to have said, to an aide placing a three-inch-high report on his desk, "That report, by its very size, demands that it will never be read."

Be sure to read what you write before you send it. Make certain capturing your point is not an exercise in endurance.

 ⊕ Take every opportunity to put positive information in writing

 ⊕ Thank and congratulate folks

 ⊕ Report on all successes, major and minor

 ⊕ Recommend solutions

 ⊕ Provide updates

When you've got something good to say, Harry Chambers says:

> "Insure accuracy, provide proof when available or necessary,
> and distribute the communication as widely as possible."[3]

Being the author of good news can put your name in a positive light when promotion time arrives, too! This has got to be good!

**Write as you speak and speak thoughtfully.
This is the best guideline for written communication at work.***

---

* Quickly upgrade your business writing skills in 10 hours. I recommend Write Well! Right now. Guaranteed. www.WriteWellInstitute.com

1. Harry E. Chambers. *Getting Promoted.* (New York: Perseus Books, 1999.)
2. Anonymous. *Owed Two A Spelling Chequer.*
3. Harry E. Chambers. Ibid.

This "telephone" has too many shortcomings to be seriously considered as a means of communication. The device is inherently of no value to us.

Western Union internal memo, 1876

I DIDN'T KNOW
THE PHONE WAS LOADED!

Ouch! I was sitting in my office one evening catching up on some e-mail when the phone rang. Even though it was well after business hours, I answered. That was my first mistake!

The "Hello" part was pleasant enough and, then, it hit!

> "What did you say to _____? I can't have you going around saying things like that. You could get me in a whole lot of trouble and I can't having you doing that. Why ever did you say that? What were you thinking? I thought I had been very clear with you and now you've gone and done _____. etc. etc."

And, all in one breath, it seemed.

For a second or two, I sat there feeling broad-sided. Whatever happened to cause this barrage? Have you ever been in a similar situation?

There was no opportunity to speak as that first stage was delivered. All accusations sounded vaguely like questions. One problem, though. No time was left for answers. She had no interest in answers. *She thought she already had them.*

Unfortunately, this is not uncommon. That is often the nature of human interactions. *You take a person's words as truthful and react and act accordingly.* That was HER first mistake!

Communication is tricky. You've probably played that game called Rumor, where one person whispers a sentence to the next person and the message makes its way around the circle. When the last person says it aloud, it often barely resembles the initial message. It is a children's game intended to be instructional.

Clear communication requires both the speaker and the listener to be fully attentive with both clarifying what they have heard until both agree on the message.

Apparently the speaker was in some way fearful. She was afraid of consequences of some kind. She was definitely more interested in passing along her fear, pain, and frustration than she was in clarifying conversation! She was clearly looking for someone to blame.

Was she interested in knowing the truth? No. Not until her fear and pain were acknowledged.

There is an important concept at work here: Whoever is most sane at the moment is responsible for the relationship. *Could you be the most sane person if you received that telephone call?*

After I recovered from the broad-siding, I responded with,

"Wow! You are really upset."

That gave her the opportunity to tell me just how upset she was. Some of the venom drained.

"Would you like to know what I did say to _____?"

That received a still angry,

"Yes, I sure would."

Then, I repeated my side of the earlier conversation.

Her response.

"Well, he said that _____."

"Is it possible that he could be mistaken?" I asked.

She apparently had not thought of that in her search for removal of her current pain. A novel idea, perhaps. She thought for a moment or two.

"Tell me again what you said," she asked.

And, I told her again.

'You're sure that's what you said?"
"Yes," I reassured her.

The penny was dropping. There really could have been another side to the conversation!

"Well, I'm going to get to the bottom of this in the morning and I'll call you then."

And, she was gone.

Whoa! How would you handle this?

For myself, I waited until she had calmed down overnight, thought better of her actions, and discussed the issue with that other guy. In that time, I sent an e-mail to the other person in the triangle, clarifying the conversation he and I had had. When the dust cleared and this issue was settled, I definitely had a conversation with the woman about how I prefer to be treated. After all, it is my responsibility to teach people how to treat me.

I slept well knowing that I did not engage in her flurry of fear nor join her in her escalating blame game. You can disengage from these types of rhino rampages too!

If your phone is loaded, be ready to disarm it!

**There's a difference between interest
and commitment. When you're
interested in doing something, you do
it only when circumstances permit.
When you're committed to something,
you accept no excuses, only results.**

Art Turock

THE QUEEN & HER BOBBLE-HEADS: EXPOSING HIDDEN AGENDAS

It all seems so nice . . . on the surface. Everyone seems to be on the same page, in the same book, yet, there is that "something" you can't quite put your finger on. It's not much, really. That person on your team or your board smiles and calmly affirms that, of course, we all want the same thing. Why doesn't it feel like that?

It's the hidden agenda. The American Heritage Dictionary says that a hidden agenda is "an undisclosed plan, especially one with an ulterior motive." The plan is often not quite as hidden as the motive and that is what bothers us.

Have you ever sat in a meeting, staring intently at a colleague, shaking your head and screaming internally,

"Why are you doing that? What is REALLY going on in that mind of yours?"

If so, you may well be facing a hidden agenda.

Recently, I was working with a board of directors of a non-profit organization. Here you would like to believe that you would find altruistic, compassionate people with high integrity. After all, they are giving their time for the good of others. NOT NECESSARILY! Most of the board members were dedicated souls committed to doing the best possible job for the organization. Three definitely were not.

After watching the board through several meetings, I became fascinated by the dynamics. One member stood out as she followed a predictable pattern: conversation on a topic proceeded, she waited like a cheetah for her moment, then sprang to her feet and suggested a radical plan. She is quick-thinking and two-faced. A poor combination! Unless you were very alert, you might not pick up the inconsistencies in her thinking, and, therefore, in her suggestions. One might call her a "convenient thinker." When it was convenient for information to be interpreted one way, she did it. Immediately requiring the information to reflect the opposite, she jumped to the other side. Due to her ability with words, she even made it seem logical to be so duplicitous.

And, she has "bobble-heads"! That's my term for people who want approval and power and think they get it from agreeing with someone who appears to have both. They don't think for themselves but align themselves with people they perceive as having power. Therefore, whenever their exalted leader makes a move, they nod in agreement without even knowing what that person has up their sleeve. Got a bobble-head or two in mind now?

Each person has their own processing time—the time it takes to fully integrate what another says and the implications of their position. When a quick-thinking, fast-talking person demands action, makes motions, and overruns the chairperson, those who process more slowly are left wondering what happened. Those left in the dust are intelligent, dedicated, interested board members, but no match for the slickster who appears to be expediting board business at a grand clip.

Many times, a flurry of emails followed those board meetings.

"What happened . . . ???"

"I felt manipulated . . . "

"I'm confused . . ."

"I don't think that was right . . ."

"Can I withdraw my seconding that motion . . . ?"

"I think we had better have another meeting."

But, the motion was made and the vote taken. Action follows and no one but the Queen and her Bobble-heads are happy. Are the bobble-heads really happy? They are as long as their fearless leader is winning. Watch how quickly they begin staring at their boots when that leader is exposed!

This particular board had been functioning with the same dynamics for years. Why? This woman had made it her business to stay on or join the board whenever it made sense for her purpose. Did she want the organization to succeed? It sounded as though she did, however, her behavior soon became transparent as I probed her thinking at meetings. I asked at one point:

> "I'm confused. You clearly said that these facts and figures supported your position and now you are saying the opposite. Which is true?"

The air was filled with her palpable grapple for words and reasons. She may be fast but she was not used to being questioned, only agreed with. Logic was unknown to her except as suited her purposes. This simple question of mine threatened her mightily with exposure of her inconsistencies and the convenience of her thinking.

What was her response? To attack me, of course. Soon she was asking for my credentials and questioning why I was hired. It only took a moment to assure her that she, in fact, had hired me for all the right reasons. Unfortunately, that logic was her undoing and she knew the jig was up . . . and so did all the other board members. Now, we could actually change the dynamics and expose and expunge the hidden power agenda. Transparency—essential in all dealings if people matter one iota—could be established.

This is an extreme case and I use it here to illustrate for you what might be going on in your office or boardroom. What followed in my work with this board was much training on two levels: communication, conflict management, and team-building skills, and collaborative decision-making processes.

What if you are faced with the Queen and her Bobble-heads? The first important step is to ask questions right at the moment you have them.

Why don't we speak up immediately? We may think the issue will become clearer if we watch and listen longer, and we don't have to risk appearing uninformed or confrontational. That is simply a matter of learning better communication skills. Asking simple questions based on information rather than emotion is the intelligent move. No need to pin anyone down on the mat. Just ask,

"It's unclear to me at this moment how those two items are related. Could you please tell me more about that?"

A simple request for information. Yes, the speaker may infer that you are missing essential brain cells, however, always remember that that is a tactic to make themselves feel superior. Just let it go by without comment and return to the logic. People with hidden agendas tend to get very upset when you do not become engaged or enraged. They want to shift the conversation to the emotional and the personal. Your intent is to keep it impersonal and focused on facts. That's an excellent first step.

Still hanging back without speaking up? Ask yourself which is worse: risking getting clarification now or living with the consequences!

Exposing hidden agendas is not always a simple matter that can be cleared up quickly and directly. Unaddressed, however, it will never go away.

Step up fearlessly and intelligently. There are people waiting to follow your lead. That makes you the leader!

DON'T MAKE EXCUSES: MAKE THINGS HAPPEN!

You know that your excuses are seldom truthful, often handy and rarely productive. So, why make them? It's no surprise that "honesty is the best policy" is so often quoted. It's the truth. So, why do we not seem to believe that it applies to the conversations we have with ourselves?

Would you feel as comfortable offering your excuses to your employer as you are offering them to yourself? Probably not. Why? Because your employer is unlikely to buy them and will probably see through them. We don't want our excuses exposed so we're careful where we proffer them. Somehow, they are quite acceptable to give to ourselves. We think they are safely hidden.

Now, does this make sense? Sure. We like to feel we can get away with things, don't we? Let ourselves off the hook. Relieve the pressure. Have some downtime. So, what's wrong with this picture?

PROMISE TO STRETCH NOT OVER-EXTEND

Folks make pie-in-the-sky goals. In a burst of enthusiasm, commitment to unrealistic goals seems possible. Take off the rose-colored glasses. *Make goals that cause you to stretch, not over-extend.*

There is a huge difference between those two positions. Stretch feels good, you know that you can do it and you know it is good for you. Over-extension causes stress, fear and exhaustion. Stretch increases your capacity slowly. You can sustain your gains. Over-extension can cause frustration, resentment, and . . . excuses.

PROMISE WHAT YOU ARE WILLING TO DELIVER

Have you ever made a promise that you knew—as you spoke—you were going to have a problem delivering? Sure you have. Why did you do it?

There ARE good reasons for doing so: You want to help someone in need. You want to work towards a promotion. You want someone to like you more, approve of you, accept you. Good reasons, but what happens when you cannot or do not deliver? All those good reasons are not only negated but you may have lost the confidence of the folks you wished to serve, please or help. Not very wise.

What about the promises you make to yourself? YOU count. *In fact, you count the most.* Why? Because *you* have to live with *you* every second. I believe that the greatest contributor to lack of self-confidence lies in our failure to keep our promises to ourselves.

Goal achievement is rooted in keeping your promises to yourself. Don't let yourself down. You'll soon find that you are able to keep your careful promises to others easily.

PROMISE NOT TO CUDDLE UP WITH YOUR APOLOGIES

It's easy to be on friendly terms with our excuses. We condition ourselves to play it safe. We limit our adventures, discoveries, interests, and risks. When we were children, this was usually not an issue. We simply went for it.

Now, I'm not suggesting throwing caution to the wind. Simply look at what holds you back. Are you, perhaps, unwilling to experience even the slightest bit of discomfort or pain? Is it possible to experience change without a little discomfort? That only happens when you change from dress shoes to bedroom slippers, or some kind person provides you with clean Huggies!

Some folks think that the safe way is to do nothing. Great! *Do you want the results that choosing to do nothing produces?* If so, you are choosing wisely. If not, choose again. **A decision to not take action is still taking action.** Be sure it makes sense for you.

Do you think that cuddling up with your apologies protects your ego? Nothing ventured, nothing risked = safety? Not so. (Remember, the saying is "nothing ventured, nothing GAINED . . . ") It's never too late to try something new. Think you're too old? Think of Grandma Moses. Think folks will laugh? Who cares? Think of the health benefits of laughter for them and proceed. Think you would fall on your face? So what? It's good exercise to pick yourself up and get going again.

**Resist the urge to make excuses that keep you from your dreams.
Don't make excuses. Make things happen!**

**Take time to deliberate, but when
the time for action has arrived, stop
thinking and go in.**

Napoleon Bonaparte

RHINO RAMPAGES:

MANAGING CONFLICT WITHOUT LOSING CO-WORKERS, CLIENTS, CREDIBILITY, OR SLEEP

**150 executives were asked:
'How often, on average, do you find
yourself responding to unexpected
crises at work?'
36% said a few times per week, while
others responded: 16%—once a day;
19%—a few times a day; 19%—a few
times a month; 9%—once a week;
1%—once a month.**

SOURCE: Accountemps, Menlo Park, CA

UNRESOLVED CONFLICT IS ORGANIZATIONAL BLOODLETTING

U nresolved conflict is like blood-letting: immediate pain, a big mess, then a slow draining while no one does anything—or worse yet, they sit around and silently watch it happen. The results can be fatal. *Slow seeping losses cannot be ignored.* On the job or in the family, they can also be deadly. We have to wake up and stop the bleeding.

You might think that the ancient practice of bloodletting has no practical application today. My father's sister was only six months old in 1922 when a prairie doctor in Canada decided that her fever would go away if she lost some blood. Not so long ago. I never knew my aunt. She died that day. The bloodletting went on too long and no one stepped in to stop the flow.

|||||||||||||||||||||||||||||||||||||||||||||||||||||||||||||||||||||||||||||||||||||||||||||||||||||||||||||||||||||||||||||||||||||||||||||||||||||||||||||||||||||||||

Graphic, yes! But, we need to pay attention. *We are too often too complacent for too long.* Profits drop, anger flares, and productivity declines when conflict is not addressed.

In his 2001 book *Conflict Resolution,* Daniel Dana states:

> "Research studies show that up to 42% of an employee's time is spent engaging in or attempting to resolve conflict."[1]

That's serious bleeding! Can you afford to lose **42% of your payroll** dollars in that way? More importantly, can you allow your own time, energy, creativity, and passion to be drained?

This is a major energy leak. Think about it. You get up on Monday morning, looking forward to a great week at work. As you're driving in, you remember that last week your co-worker managed to take the credit for the work the two of you did together. (Energy leak.) Then, you remember the look that co-worker gave you across the table as she spoke of her success. The look said, "Don't make a scene. Let me have this one." (Energy leak.) You notice the feelings of anger, betrayal, shock, and unfairness that ran through your body at that time. (Energy leak.) You begin to dread seeing her in twenty minutes. (Energy leak.)

Sound familiar? Sure. Things happen at work. **Ambition leaps over integrity. It's not pretty AND it needs to be addressed.** Donald Trump's reality TV show, *The Apprentice,* showed how cracks in the integrity shield start. At first, all players were focused on their team winning. As the show progressed, it had to come down to only one person winning. Did ambition leap over integrity? Did the dogs eat the dogs until only one remained alive? This supposed insight into the workings of big business cannot be allowed to translate well into the day-to-day operations of the average organization.

On the whole, people have to learn to play nicely together at work. The question is, who's teaching them? When I go into an organization where folks are at each other's throats, it's often very late in the game.

> They are screaming, *"Fix this mess!"* Usually, that means, *"Fix the other guy!"* or *"Make my employee relations problems go away!"* Freely translated, it means *"Remove this pain and make my life easier."*

The energy leaks have turned into a flood. No one can pay attention to the work because they are being swept up in the current tidal wave. There's anxiety, anger, irritability, and fear. The organization or department is bleeding to death. You need a tourniquet immediately and a strategy for removing unnecessary sharp objects from the workplace.

THE TOURNIQUET

Call in an outside expert. By the time conflict has escalated to severe blood loss, you need expert help—a 911 business call. Save the employee. Save the company. Do it now . . . call me, 760.735.8686.

A manager, or even the CEO, is too invested in an immediate fix to understand the patients' pain, diagnose the situation, and negotiate a remedy. They are too close to the blood. They want to sew 'em up and get 'em back on the front lines—a surgical solution. That's a short-term gain leading to long-term pain.

A hired consultant can apply a tourniquet and stop the blood flow. It is important to get someone outside of the "feelings mix," as that is what complicates using inside help. The outside expert is in a much better position to see all sides, mediate the issues, and insure a solution more focused on the overall health and wellness of the company. And, that is the focus of the expert's work. She is not trying to run a company, meet deadlines, oversee operations, AND mediate a conflict. She's there to fix the problem.

THE REMEDY

Certainly, a tourniquet is a quick fix but that's not all that's needed. According to Webster, a *remedy* is "something that corrects or counteracts a disease or condition." That's where the progressive, successful organizations shine.

Workplace conflict can have very high costs. There has been a huge increase in employment lawsuits, in recent years. In the mix of wrongful termination, discrimination, and sexual harassment—AND all the slights, disputes, squabbles, and power struggles leading up to them—you have a recipe for low morale, increased absenteeism, and down-turned productivity. Then, add the tendency of people to rush to court. Your workplace then is filled with fear and the courts are teeming with litigation. Talk about a major energy leak!

So, the damage is done and the tourniquet is in place. The pressure is off. This is a dangerous stage because you might drift off into unconsciousness; you think the problem has been abated and you turn your attention to other urgent things.

Wake up! The problem is still there. The wound is still seeping. No healing is taking place.

Wherever people work together, conflict arises. Pro-active conflict management and communication training is the preventative solution. That's simple. If your organization is thinking that such training is a waste of time and money, think of the 42% of an employee's time that is spent engaging in or attempting to resolve conflict.

Can you possibly afford *not* to train your people? Of course not, and, the sooner the better.

Train your people all at once? Although it is the best solution as it creates a level playing field of skill-development and provides structured opportunities to discuss the issues, it is not always possible to shut down your operation. If that's true, train them all within a very short period of time. Don't leave anyone at a disadvantage due to a lack of training.

Bill Gates says that

"Education is the best preparation for being able to adapt."

Educate yourself. Educate your people.

You simply do not have 42% of the expertise, experience, energy, time and creativity to lose every day!

---

1. Daniel Dana. *Conflict Resolution: Mediation Tools for Everyday Worklife*. (New York: McGraw Hill Briefcase Books, 2001).

RHINO REALITY:
||||||||||||||||||||||||||||||||||||||||||||

RHINOS ARE TRANSLOCATED OFTEN
TO PROTECT THEM.

RULES FOR RECOGNIZING RHINOS:
||||||||||||||||||||||||||||||||||||||||||||||||||||||||||||||||||||||||||||||||||

NO ONE WANTS TO FIRE THEM SO THEY ARE
SHIPPED FROM DEPARTMENT TO DEPARTMENT.

**Up to 30% of a typical manager's time
is spent dealing with conflict.**

K. Thomas and W. Schmidt[1]

ARE YOU USING THESE THREE WAYS TO MISMANAGE CONFLICT?

Conflict is a daily occurrence in all areas of life. No one is exempt. No relationship is without it. I believe even a human and his or her clone would manage to find strong differences of perception, perspective or values!

Writing about disputes makes good copy. Just check your local newspaper or late-night news program. Who is doing what to whom is the news! The more horrific, the better, it seems. It's the stuff gossip is made of, as well.

Conflict management skills are learned. You're not born with them, they're learned by interacting with others while you're growing up, most specifically when you're a teenager. You watch how others handle conflict, then test out your own versions of those behaviors and determine which ones work for you—get you what you want—and which ones lead to more

||||||||||||||||||||||||||||||||||||||||||||||||||||||||||||||||||||||||||||||||||||||||||||||||||||||||||||||||||||||||||||||||||||||||||||||||||

difficulty. So, if you find that what you've learned so far is not working . . . it would be wise to learn new, constructive, useful, effective ones.

In theory, the parties involved in a conflict have many ways to respond to or resolve their issue. In actuality, three ways prevail: avoidance, withholding, and violence. All three do nothing to turn the confrontation into communication. In fact, they are guaranteed to do just the opposite.

AVOIDANCE

"If I don't say anything, there will be no conflict." Not so. Your breath gets short, your stomach churns and your shoulders live permanently at your earlobes. The conflict has not disappeared—you are wearing it! And, suffering.

Certainly, there are times when avoidance works. Everyone occasionally has a bad day. That is a good time to use avoidance. The problem is short-lived. Most people know what caused it. They care enough about the person to stay out of their way for a day or so. Wise choice. It's best to avoid them.

If they have more bad than good days, though, that needs to be talked about. Exerting control over others in your environment by expecting them to adjust to your bad moods is tyranny.

Avoiders often appear to be compliant and accepting. They smile. They cooperate. They rock no boats. Inwardly, they are seething. If they have low self-esteem, they may even blame themselves for their perceived inability to get along with the tyrant. They need practical skills for expressing their points of view.

If you are using avoidance as your primary conflict management strategy, how is it working for you?

- ✦ How's your health?
- ✦ Your level of frustration?
- ✦ Your self-esteem?
- ✦ Your self-confidence?

Avoiding conflict at all costs will directly impact those parts of your life, whether you choose to acknowledge it or not. Take a close look and carefully consider your answer about whether or not you are an "avoider". You could save yourself from serious illness or emotional breakdown—and improve your relationships at the same time!

WITHHOLDING

Withholding takes place when you do not want to address the conflict but you want another person to know you are angry, upset or disappointed. You simply do not give the person what they want or need. You ignore them when they speak, or, purposefully misunderstand them. You do the minimum required, less than you are capable of. The silent treatment is a form of withholding, too. You refuse to speak to the person with whom you have the conflict or unmet need.

Does this approach work? It may get you the response you want in the short-term, however, in the long-term it fails miserably . . . especially in the workplace. All it does there is escalate the conflict.

A popular form of withholding is *triangulating*—which means not being direct with the person with whom you have the dispute but attempting to go through a third person. All that does is draw that third person, who would probably rather not be involved at all, into the conflict as a go-between. It does not solve the conflict, and in fact can make it worse. The thing with disputes, complaints, and gripes is that you have to *tell someone who can actually do something about it*. Otherwise, it is simply gossip and venting. You have to be careful. Your reputation is on the line . . . and your job may be as well.

In the workplace, you may have a supervisor who is willing and trained to help. No matter what though, any employer or supervisor will be much happier if you work out differences yourself. That requires skill, and, fortunately, those skills can be learned.

VIOLENCE

"Between 1993 and 1999 in the United States, an average of 1.7 million violent victimizations per year were committed against persons who were at work or on duty, according to the National Crime Victimization Survey (NCVS). Workplace violence accounted for 18% of all violent crime during the 7-year period."[2] The good news is that violent crimes have declined since 1993. There are still far too many.

The Canadian Center for Occupational Health & Safety defines workplace violence as " . . . *any act in which a person is abused, threatened, intimidated or assaulted in his or her employment.*"[3] Workplace violence includes:

- ✤ **threatening behavior** such as shaking fists, destroying property, or throwing objects;
- ✤ **verbal or written threats**: any expression of an intent to inflict harm;
- ✤ **harassment**: any behavior that demeans, embarrasses, humiliates, annoys, alarms, or verbally abuses a person and that is known to be or would be expected to be unwelcome (this includes words, gestures, intimidation, bullying, or other inappropriate activities);
- ✤ **verbal abuse**: swearing, insults, or condescending language;
- ✤ **physical attacks**: hitting, shoving, pushing, or kicking.

Many state governments and corporations have strongly-worded policies regarding workplace violence. According to an American Society of Industrial Security survey, the top strategy indicated by respondents for preventing workplace violence is employee training.

As a conflict management expert, I agree. Pro-active companies address the high cost of day-to-day conflict in the workplace. When I offer training in conflict and anger management, negotiation, mediation, and communication, executives and their staffs learn and practice the skills they need to feel competent, confident, and yes, comfortable enough, to handle conflict effectively. And as a bonus, the training affects the quality of life for each person in all situations. **Happier, healthier employees = Greater productivity.** It's not rocket science!

A zero tolerance policy is imperative for every single workplace. Nothing less should be tolerated.

**Violence is simply unacceptable.
We need to feel . . . and be . . . safe at work.**

1. K. Thomas and W. Schmidt. *A survey of managerial interests with respect to conflict.* (Academy of Management Journal, June 1976.)
2. Detis T. Duhart, Ph.D. *Bureau of Justice Statistics Special Report.* (National Crime Victimization Survey, December 2001, NCJ 190076) http://www.ojp.usdoj.gov
3. The Canadian Center for Occupational Health & Safety. Hamilton, Ontario, www.ccohs.ca

RHINO REALITY:
|||||||||||||||||||||||||||||||||||||||||||||

PRIOR TO THE INITIAL ENCOUNTER, THE RHINO LOWERS ITS HEAD, SCREAMS, AND PAWS THE EARTH.

RULES FOR RECOGNIZING RHINOS:
|||||||||||||||||||||||||||||||||||||||||||||||||||||||||||||||||||||||||||||||||||||||||||

RHINOS AT WORK FLASH SIGNS OF AN IMPENDING CHARGE.

**More people would learn from their
mistakes if they weren't so busy
denying that they made them.**

Anonymous

IS A NUDGE IS MORE EFFECTIVE THAN A SHOVE?

A dam was part of a two-person team responsible for negotiating company-wide salary increases. Trina sat next to him, completing the team. The CEO and CFO represented management and there was one voice from the venture capitalists.

Adam sat at the table after two very long hours, jacket off, ready to pounce. He was tired, worn-down, and fed-up. Health benefits were the final issue. It had been left to the end because of the huge difference of opinion as to who was really responsibile for it. The conversation heated up. Adam, hot under the collar, had had enough. He leaned forward to speak, rising to the bait, exasperation oozing from every pore. Trina, observing the sparks, was determined to keep the fire under control. She nudged Adam, saying, "We're doing well. Let's sit back and listen a little longer." Adam relaxed. Management spoke. Their offer was close to reasonable. Two quick volleys and the deal was done. A nudge saved the day . . . and the health care of one hundred families! It was a nudge in the right direction.

PRACTICE THE GENTLE ART OF NUDGING

Are you more motivated by a nudge or a shove? Probably we've all been motivated by both. One is easier to hear and accept. By definition, to nudge someone is "to seek the attention of; to prod lightly; to urge into action". That sounds gentle . . . and positive.

You've heard that you'll catch more flies with honey than with vinegar. It's true. We are generally under-appreciated and over-criticized. When we're offered honey, we're hungry for it and it is much more palatable than vinegar. Who enjoys someone's acid tongue raining down criticism? I'll take dripping praise, recognition, and acknowledgment over that any day, won't you?

Unfortunately, manure also seems to be a fly magnet so that may be where the metaphor runs out. It does remind us, though, to be sure that our appreciation and intentions are genuine because any other kind smells!

Nudging is catching people doing things right! Use your time and energy for moving the positive forward.

Remember my piano teacher who told me to keep making beautiful music and let the bad notes fall on the floor? Each time I played the piece I was careful to have fewer bad notes because she reminded me to focus on the music, not the mistakes. **Catch people doing things right.** (I can't say this often enough because it's impact is enormous!) You'll feel better with your focus on the positive. They'll respond and give you more of what you want.

I'm not suggesting denial. Things do need improving and they need to be talked about. If, however, your focus is on encouraging rather than discouraging, you'll see a significant increase in the behaviors you prefer. Remember that William James quote:

> "The deepest craving of the human nature is the need to feel appreciated."

So, get out the honey and catch them flies! Nudge them in the right direction and things will go faster.

PRACTICE THE JUDICIOUS USE OF THOUGHTFUL SHOVING

The problem with shoving in general is that it is too careless, too thoughtless, and too often a knee-jerk reaction. It can be a *street-fighter* strategy that leaves your victim bleeding and stunned. Although usually not a felony, it should be. So, no street-fighting! And, we do need to know what to do when a nudge is insufficient and a death blow is too severe.

I was shoved once . . . and hard. I was twelve years old and I was called to the principal's office on Awards Day. Being a top student, president of this-and-that, an accomplished musician and an all-around asset to the school, I was certain that the principal, Mr. Martin, simply wanted to tell me personally how much he appreciated my efforts.

Imagine my surprise when he said,

> "Well, young lady, you are at the top of your game around here in many ways and you'll receive the awards to prove it. We have to give them to you, but we don't want to. You think too much of yourself and it shows. So, take my advice, fix the attitude. You're destined for success, but you'll be sidetracked by your attitude."

I felt like I had been shoved against the wall by a Mack truck! Was it effective? Was it the truth? YES, on both counts. Thinking back, several teachers had tried to nudge me towards that truth, but I was not listening. It took the big shove to wake me up.

Mr. Martin was a kind man with my best interests at heart. It took something out of him to exert the force required to turn my head in the right direction. He knew when to shove . . . and how. Don't shove unless you have excellent communication skills and a clearly thought-out strategy.

Shoving from anger creates injury. Unless you are willing to terminate the relationship, you need honest, kind communication—and the skills to manage conflict—if you want a healthy result from a shove. Be sure you learn these things before you push your weight around. Without them, you will be a bully or a bull in a china shop!

Know when to nudge, know when to shove, but first, know when to appreciate.

Rhoberta Shaler, PhD

'Tis the business of little minds to
shrink; but he whose heart is firm,
and whose conscience approves his
conduct, will pursue his principles
unto death.

Thomas Paine

GOOD BOUNDARIES
MAKE GOOD NEIGHBORS.

D o you have good boundaries? Do you clearly know the limit or edge that defines you as separate from others? Your skin marks the limit of your physical self, however, there are other boundaries that extend well beyond your skin. You become aware of those when someone stands too close. That's when someone comes inside that invisible circle known as your *comfort zone*.

Boundaries can be somewhat flexible. It may be fine for your lover to stand much closer to you than most of your friends or your workplace colleagues. A friend can stand closer than a stranger. When someone is angry or hostile towards you, you might want to keep quite a distance from him or her!

At work, boundary issues are very important. I was recently talking with a friend who had taken a theater class with his wife. During the course, the subject of "the talk" was discussed. The talk is the conversation two actors have before they play scenes requiring intimacy or fighting. They discuss what is OK with them, and what is not, so they do not overstep one another's boundaries inadvertently.

My friend, a director of a community college, decided it would be a good idea to have the talk with his entire staff. In doing so, many helpful things came to light. One person on his team said that having anyone closer to him that four feet was extremely uncomfortable. Another said it was no problem for them to be very close. Each had different needs for feeling safe. Some have different cultural norms for comfort zones. What are yours? Do you express them at work? Do you take responsibility for teaching people how to treat you?

There are other kinds of boundaries—emotional, spiritual, sexual, and relational. You know the limits of what feels safe and appropriate for you. Do you maintain good boundaries that keep you

feeling safe? Emotional boundaries, for example, honor the set of feelings and reactions that are distinctly yours. You respond to the world uniquely based on your perceptions, history, values, goals, and concerns. You can find people who react to the world in similar ways as you, but no one will react precisely as you do in all ways. That is your uniqueness.

Your spiritual boundaries are set when you know the right spiritual path for yourself. If someone tries to tell you that their truth is a little more true than yours, you can draw the line.

There is so much in the news about violence and sexual aggression. Sexual boundaries must be clear. You, and only you, choose with whom you interact sexually—and the extent of that interaction. All relationships that are healthy have boundaries that are respected. The roles you play in each relationship need to come with clear limits of what you consider to be appropriate and healthy interaction.

Are you taking good care of yourself? Can you clearly tell another person where your boundaries are and what the consequences of crossing them are, in ways that move the relationships forward? Sometimes that movement forward will strengthen your bond, sometimes it will end it.

Boundaries bring your life into order. Holding your boundaries exercises your right to define yourself and your relationships to others.

You teach people how to treat you and you are 100% responsible for doing so. Clarity is up to you.

RHINO REALITY:
‖‖‖‖‖‖‖‖‖‖‖‖‖‖‖‖‖‖‖‖‖‖‖‖‖‖‖‖‖‖‖‖‖‖‖‖‖‖‖

RHINOS AGGRESSIVELY AND VIGOROUSLY DEFEND THEIR TURF AGAINST RIVALS.

RULES FOR RECOGNIZING RHINOS:
‖‖‖

THEY ARE OFTEN TOO INSECURE, NEUROTIC, FEARFUL, AND UNCOMFORTABLE TO PLAY NICELY IN THE COMPANY SANDBOX.

Discussion is an exchange of knowledge; argument, an exchange of ignorance.

Robert Quillen

DRAW THE LINE IN
THE SAND IN INK

W e are one hundred percent responsible for teaching people how to treat us. I've said it often because it is true . . . and most folks don't get it!

If someone tells a racist joke in front of you and it is something you do not appreciate, you must say something. *If you do not,* you have just told the joke teller that it is all right with you. It's that easy!

One reason people do not speak up is their fear of conflict. Does that make sense to you? Not many people were ever given careful, specific training in handling conflict effectively. They shy away from speaking up when a friend, co-worker, or family member offends them. Speaking up on your own behalf requires confidence in your communication skills. You have to believe that you deserve to be respected. And of course, the rest of that most basic equation is that you treat others with respect as well.

As we've already discussed, a boundary is a limit or edge that defines us as separate from others. Setting boundaries with the folks closest to us is essential to creating healthy relationships. We have physical boundaries as well as emotional, spiritual, sexual and social ones. When our emotional or social boundaries are trespassed upon, we feel vulnerable and uncomfortable. That's the time to speak up.

How does this translate to the workplace? Work involves different people with differing levels of responsibility, expertise, and experience. You may have a supervisor or manager, as well as folks who work under you.

How do you set boundaries with your boss? Big question, as that is likely the first person you do not want to offend. Communication skills to the rescue!

Breathe

First, take a deep breath in through your nose and let it slowly out through your mouth. Relax. One big mistake that is often made is reacting rather than responding when someone crosses your boundaries. It is just that very reactivity that scares us, and rightly so. When you are reactive, you are dangerous to yourself and your relationships. Reactivity is often thoughtless. That's not the way to improve relationships.

Take the time to center yourself—to relax and think—before speaking up.

Identify

Identify the cause of your discomfort. Was it the words said to you, the tone of voice, the timing, the company, or the inappropriateness of the comment? Then, identify how you have responded to it on a feeling level. Are you feeling frustrated, hurt, or scared? Those are the underlying emotions of the arousal we call anger. Begin there to figure out your feelings and your response. There is no point confronting someone until you are clear about what you're feeling, why you're feeling it, and what you are going to say.

Clarify your thoughts and feelings
before speaking up.

Choose

Both the words *and* the timing are important if your boundary setting is to be effective. Of course, you will want to remember the Golden Rule. You do not want to become the offender when your true desire is to request a change in behavior.

Laura was participating in a team meeting. When she was asked for her report, she presented it in a very detailed fashion. The manager apparently thought that it was too lengthy. She raised her voice and said,

> "You can't be wasting our time blathering on with all those details. Just give us the facts, the bottom line, and don't be running off at the mouth. I expect my people to be concise."

Laura was embarrassed, belittled, and put-down in front of her peers. She fell silent for the duration of the meeting. Naturally, she was upset. And, she was angry. What did she now need to do? The first smart thing she did was not REACT.

Maintain the presence of mind necessary to not react when conflict arises. It will save you much pain, frustration, embarassment, and regret later on.

Speak Up

Fortunately, Laura did not fall into the trap of complaining to her team members after the meeting. She calmed herself down and went to see her manager. Laura began the conversation by saying that she was sorry her desire to give a full report on her work was interpreted as time-wasting. The manager indicated that she was glad that Laura now knew better.

Laura proceeded to state how she wanted to be treated in future. *That is the bold step required.* How that step is taken makes all the difference.

"It is important to me to do well and to have productive, respectful relationships with my team members. I felt put down and belittled in the meeting. I would appreciate being told about any mistakes, shortcomings, or unmet expectations in private. Would you help me do a better job by agreeing to do that?"

Notice that Laura did not place any blame, make any judgments, or display anger in her statement. She owned her feelings and offered a guideline for the relationship. She did not react. She responded thoughtfully and clearly: **quick, direct communication ending with a request for agreement.**

Laura was teaching her manager how she wanted to be treated. She did it respectfully. She stood up for herself. She drew a boundary gently and clearly. Is there any question in the manager's mind regarding how Laura wants to be treated? Likely not.

Whether or not the matter ends there is another question. Sometimes, boundary statements have to be repeated several times before they are honored. Sometimes, they are not honored at all. Then, it is time for the next step.

Make A Decision

If the manager berated Laura in front of her team on other subsequent occasions, she would then have a decision to make.

She would be wise to step back and get a better perspective on her work, her team, and the company. It is important for Laura to first examine her work. If all is well except for this one relationship, she might choose to accept that the manager will not change. If she finds the relationship intolerable, she might ask for a transfer or find another position.

We are responsible for teaching people how to treat us. (Can I say this often enough?) We cannot coerce them into treating us how we wish. How people respond to our boundary setting is a function of two important concepts:

✦   their own self-confidence, and

✦   their perceived value of the relationship.

If Laura's manager demonstrates her own lack of self-confidence by repeatedly needing a scapegoat, she will likely not change her behavior. The manager *will* likely respond positively to Laura's request, if she wants to keep Laura's specialized expertise and talent on the team.

Are there any relationships in your life where boundaries have slipped and need shoring up? Follow these few steps. You'll build confidence and gain respect.

Let people know who you are and where you stand.
Draw your lines in the sand in ink.

The people to fear are not those who disagree with you, but those who disagree with you and are too cowardly to let you know.

Napoleon Bonaparte

RHINO REALITY:

RHINOS LEAVE HEAPS OF DUNG WHICH THEY SPREAD SIX FEET WIDE TO MARK THEIR TERRITORY.

RULES FOR RECOGNIZING RHINOS:

IT'S HARD TO WANT TO GET CLOSE TO A RHINO.

**It is better to ask some of the
questions than know all the answers.**

James Thurber

PRIOR TO CLEARING THE AIR. . .

So, the conversation has begun. You listen and ask for more information even when you are not sure you want it. You ask because your desire to understand the other person is greater than your fear of hearing what they have to say. Why? Because you want the relationship to improve. That's the whole point of having this conversation.

What now? Are you clear about what you need and want? Can you clearly state it so that the other person can understand? Remember, communication means the information is being transmitted AND received in BOTH directions. Clarify your thinking before entering an important conversation. Sometimes it happens that you unexpectedly find yourself in such a conversation. At those times, you have the right to say,

> "This issue is very important to me and I would like to talk about this with you. I would like to gather my thoughts and discuss this at _____ time."

Stating you would like time to consider the issue demonstrates respect for yourself and for the other person.

When anger is present, postpone the conversation until calmer heads prevail. You know that when you are angry, as Lawrence J. Peter says, you are likely to make "the best speech you'll ever regret". Be wise. Calm down first. It is important to let the other person know when you are angry.

Anger is natural and healthy. It is simply an arousal in the body giving you information that your boundaries have been crossed and you feel discounted, frustrated, hurt, or scared. Anger, then, is a kind of barometer, and it is good. What you do with that anger, however, is a choice. It is important to let folks know when you feel it, but it can be destructive to speak in the heat of the moment.

What happens in a working or intimate relationship when the air needs to be cleared? You are distracted. Your productivity, focus, and balance are affected. Perhaps you are feeling frustrated or disrespected, and you want to convey those feelings so things can improve. Perhaps there is a touchy issue that simply must be addressed. This is the trickiest of conversations and therefore it needs special attention.

First big step. Wait until you are not angry. You want the greatest possibility for this to be a learning conversation, right? Sure, you might want and need to work that upset out of your body. Go for a fast walk. Play squash. Do tae-bo. Move that energy and dissipate it—then you're ready to talk.

Second big step. Be respectful. Ask the other person if this is a good time to talk to them about something you would like their help with. If it is not, ask for a specific time when the conversation can take place. This demonstrates respect for the other person and the importance of the conversation to you.

Next, take the time to lay out the issue.

> "When _____ happens, I find I feel _____. I would like to feel _____ and I think that could happen if _____. Would you/ could you help me with that by ____?"

Now, LISTEN! Listening means that your head *and* your ears are working together.

- You are not composing what you are going to say next while the other person is talking.
- You are not refuting their words in your head.
- You are not trying to top their story.
- You ARE listening.

Particularly in an intimate relationship, you can be sure that both of you are affected when one of you is upset before an issue is even aired. If that is not the case, question whether your relationship is even close!

Your "negotiating partner" knows you are listening when you ask questions that indicate your interest in understanding the issue. Hopefully, those same kinds of questions will also come your way. *This is communicating.* You are deepening the relationship by understanding the thoughts and feelings of the other person.

"Can we talk?" can be a welcome question. If it is an opening gambit to launch a lecture, you'll soon lose your audience. Use your skills to make it an opportunity to learn, and an opportunity to enrich your relationships.

Be wise. Take the time to calm yourself before any "big" conversations. You'll reduce your chances of making the greatest speech you'll ever regret.

**A wise man is superior to any insults
which can be put upon him, and the
best reply to unseemly behavior is
patience and moderation.**

Molière

WRESTLING RHINOS: DEALING WITH DIFFICULT PEOPLE

L et's face it. For a minute or two, every so often, every one of us is someone else's idea of a "difficult person." There are, however, folks who make a lifestyle of being difficult. At least, that's the way it seems to us . . . and maybe to a few other people in our offices.

A difficult person is one whose behavior causes *you* a problem. It could be a boss, a co-worker, a client, or customer. It is unlikely that you will be able to change that person's behavior, however, you are entirely able to wisely manage your part of your interactions with him or her. That is your most effective strategy in dealing with difficult people. That is where you will find your power in those situations.

Now, before you can tackle these difficult people, *it is essential to have your own act together.* Is there any tiny chance that your actions, words, or behaviors actually contribute to the other person's difficult behavior? Remember, someone who is difficult in your perception, may not be seen as difficult to others.

Ever had a morning like this? You're short on sleep. You're running a little late. You ran out of coffee. You almost missed your bus. You forgot your briefcase and your lunch. You get to work just in time to make it to a very important meeting. The only available chair is next to the person you like least and, as you slip into it as unobtrusively as possible, he leans over and says sarcastically and none too quietly,

"Nice you could make it."

Is he being a difficult person? Perhaps. Especially if you could have predicted his remark. The telling reality comes when you draw your next breath and open your mouth. *What do you say?*

If you have the presence of mind to ignore the sarcasm and respond with a genuine "Thank you," then you're not going to have much trouble with anyone. If, however, your blood pressure soars, your hands grow clammy, and you begin to sputter . . . he's got you. If *"Jerk"* is the only thing you can mutter, he got precisely the effect he wanted. What did you get?

First, when you think you're dealing with a difficult person, look in the mirror. **How are you behaving in the situation?** Collect yourself. Decide on your behavior strategy. Stay in control of yourself and you're likely to stay in control of the situation.

PATTERNS OF DIFFICULT BEHAVIOR

⊹ **Some folks are bullies.** They bombard you with their aggression, make cutting remarks and get angry when things are not to their liking.

⊹ **Some folks are whiners and complainers.** They seldom take action to change things because they prefer to find fault.

⊹ **Some stay silent or uncommunicative.** Often they seem to have vocabularies of one-syllable responses—"Yep," "No," or a grunt.

✦ **Some agree with everything you say.** They express their willingness to be supportive, however, they seldom follow through. Often they are labeled passive-aggressive, and they are!

✦ **Some are simply constant wet blankets.** Nothing will ever work. Everything is impossible. Expect the worst because it will likely happen. That's their credo.

✦ **Some simply know everything** . . . or think they do. They are condescending, imposing, pompous, and dismissive. Their mission in life seems to be to make you feel like a fool.

✦ **Some cannot make a decision, or at least, they *will* not.** They wait for decisions to be made for them. Often, these are perfectionists.

These are the categories that Robert Bramson created in his book, *Coping with Difficult People*[1]. Do they sound familiar? Sure, very few people are constantly difficult—especially if they want something from you—however, there are some basic strategies that will help when you are confronted with difficult behaviors.

ACKNOWLEDGE UNDERLYING FEELINGS & THINK OF DESIRED RESULTS

A customer is yelling at you about a missing order (report, product, etc.). Take a breath and say,

> "I understand that this has created a difficulty for you and we want to find a way to resolve it for you as quickly as possible."

That may be a translation of what you are *really* thinking, which may be:

> "You are being abusive, loud and unreasonable and I want you to go away."

No matter. You have spoken about your feelings and acknowledged the customer's as well. You have shown both your maturity and your willingness to provide customer service, even if that sentence is a wise translation of

> "Listen up, jerk. You have no right to yell at me. No one pays me enough to be yelled at."

It is not the conversation in your head that you need to be concerned with when you deal with difficult people. It is the actual words that come out of your mouth. Even in your relationships at home, you are well aware of what pushes peoples' buttons and what appeases them.

> RULE: **Before doing or saying anything to anyone, imagine the result you want from the conversation and say only things that take you in that direction.**

USE LANGUAGE WELL

Another phrase that allows you to glide out of situations that could escalate is

"You could be right."

Why waste energy arguing with someone who knows it all? They are looking for confirmation of their brilliance, their perfect worldview, and their authority. Unless it is a matter of life and breath for your job, consider genuinely saying, "You could be right." It costs you nothing, appeases the other, and your blood pressure remains low.

If you happen to be thinking that this is less than honest, it isn't. The possibility does exist that the other person is correct. It may be remote, but it does exist.

> RULE: **Maintain your sense of self and center by acknowledging others and avoiding energy drains.**

BE FLEXIBLE—ALLOW FOR DIFFERENCES

Everyone does not think as you do. That's no surprise. Take the time to ask good questions and listen to others without judgment. Most folks have compelling reasons for their beliefs and behaviors, and they are entitled to them. Be sure that you have not become inflexible and intolerant. Tension does that to people.

In the name of efficiency, folks forget they are talking to other folks who also have lives and feelings. *Be sure that you put people first.*

Give pressure a name. Preface your remarks with,

> "I know that I am feeling pressured and you are likely feeling that way, too."

Ask how you can best manage situations together . . . and listen. As Zig Ziglar reminds us:

> "When we are more concerned with helping people get what they want, our wants will likely be met."

Take a deep breath and exhale slowly before answering anyone when you feel tense. That will keep you from *being* the difficult person! Imagine the result you want from the interaction five minutes from now. What might feel good at the moment may cause you untold weeks of rebuilding five minutes from now.

RULE: Choose your words and actions wisely.

BE WILLING TO TEACH PEOPLE HOW TO TREAT YOU

When difficult people cannot be side-stepped, practice communicating your boundaries clearly. When you feel your pulse quickening, remember the earlier advice: make an "I" statement quickly. With a little expert turn, you can acknowledge the other person and set your boundary simultaneously:

I-STATEMENT: What I need, feel, see, hear, think, believe . . .

> "When _____ happens, I feel _____ because _____. What I would like to feel is _____ and _____ would help me do that.

OR

> "I think that I can help you get what you want. I need your help to do that by (reviewing the facts, stepping back and allowing me some space, speaking quietly so that I can assimilate your needs, etc.) Can that happen?"

There are some folks with whom you work who will persistently push your buttons. They may be unaware of their poor social skills. They may be miserable by nature. They may only have a sense of power in their lives when they are pushing people around. Who knows? The *reason* they are doing what they are doing is less important than how you manage their effect on you.

This is where boundary-setting becomes imperative! Ask the person out for coffee. Gulp! Yes, actually plan to spend a little time with them. Then, using only "I" statements—that means not using "You" as the subject of ANY sentence that you speak—explain what is bothering you and what you would like to have changed. Then, ask for their cooperation. That's the difficult part. It's like asking for the sale. Most folks balk right there. You have to take this to its logical conclusion. Ask them if they are willing to honor and respect your boundary, your needs. If they are not, then be prepared to tell them what your next step will be. Go upline if necessary, however, explain to him or her that you would prefer to handle it between yourselves.

If the problem is your boss or supervisor, things change slightly. Before requesting your little heart-to-heart, do your homework. Be prepared with specific examples of interactions that upset you and use them as examples of times when you were unable to do your work efficiently and productively. Demonstrate to them the benefits of changing their behavior around you.

Does this sound like something you could do? I hope so. What are the benefits (to you or to the company) of living with frustration, fear, and tension on a daily basis? Take action on your own behalf.

> RULE: **Ask clearly for what you need and want. Be willing to hear yes or no, and make a plan based on each contingency.**

KNOW YOUR OWN BOTTOM LINE

Everything in life has a cost. Know your own bottom line. Think of your life as one whole piece. If you find practical ways of managing relationships with difficult folks, you will not be irritable and short with the people you love at home. If you do not or cannot find the way, what is the price?

Knowing when to hold and when to fold is wise. Sometimes you simply have to communicate your bottom line and be willing to pay the price it demands.

"If this cannot be changed, I will find other employment" may have to come from your mouth.

"If we cannot find a way to talk about things equitably, I will have to take the issue to the manager" may be necessary.

"If the sniping, gossip, stealing, lying, slurring, trashing, yelling continues, you will be fired" may be the next step.

You have choice when confronted with difficult behavior. Remember, there is a person under that behavior who is wanting to be understood. That person is generally fearful and lacking in self-esteem. If you can overlook the overt behavior and dig a little, you'll likely find someone who simply needs much reassurance that they are OK. Sometimes, you do not have the time, energy, or willingness to do this. Only you can decide.

You are not powerless in the face of difficult behavior. Choose to take action. You'll feel better and things will change more quickly. That's the result you want, isn't it?

RULE: **Know your bottom line!**

1. Bramson, Robert. *Coping With Difficult People.* (New York: Anchor Press/Doubleday, 1981).

How many a dispute could have been deflated into a single paragraph if the disputants had dared to define their terms?

Aristotle

RULES OF ENGAGEMENT FOR DIFFICULT CONVERSATIONS

Do you avoid difficult conversations? You know, the ones you would rather not have to have. Research shows that many folks will even leave their positions and walk away rather than manage the interpersonal conflicts at work.

Difficult conversations are like walking in minefields. You're stepping very carefully. You're paying attention. You're aware, even hyper-vigilant, and there is still the possibility of KA-BOOM! Unless you have a detailed map of the minefield, you are anxious, uncertain, and intimidated by the potential for harm.

What is the purpose of minefields?
To deter folks from coming closer.

That is why so many folks avoid difficult conversations. **Avoidance may create a sense of safety, but it creates a danger, too.** Without the ability to sweep the minefield, no progress can be made toward the goal! Sweeping the minefield demonstrates your willingness and desire to move forward. Sweeping, though, requires courage.

Good communication skills are like a metal detector in a minefield. They allow you to sweep the area looking for previously undetected danger zones. Once found, the operator can probe around the sensitive area to see how far it extends. Then, the object can be carefully exposed to reveal its true form and color. It may be simply an errant piece of shrapnel from a previous engagement, or, a real mine protecting personal or professional territory. By proceeding with great skill, no one will get hurt.

Good mine detection skills give you the confidence to walk in minefields unscathed.

Good communication skills give you the confidence to have difficult conversations.

RULES OF ENGAGEMENT FOR DIFFICULT CONVERSATIONS

1. Listen rather than hear.
2. Honestly endeavor to understand the opposition first.
3. Be clear about what you think and want.
4. Invest time in preparation.
5. Be willing to engage and go the extra mile.
6. Understand the skills required for adequate self-defense.
7. Understand the difference between self-defense and defensiveness.
8. Choose appropriate timing.
9. Remain engaged.

10. Believe that peace is possible as even an agreed upon truce is peaceful.

Listen Rather Than Hear

The difference between hearing and listening is the difference between memorizing a recipe and eating. You can recite the recipe aloud but you still do not have the flavor!

Listening is dangerous. You cannot do it without engaging with the other person. It involves empathy and feeling. Listen only if you care about the person or about the relationship. Otherwise, hearing is adequate.

Hearing is done every moment of the day. Listening requires attention and effort. When you are truly listening, you are picking up both the verbal and the non-verbal communication, integrating the information, and feeding back your understanding of the message. *Listening takes intention, willingness, caring and courage.*

Honestly Endeavor To Understand The Opposition

We are all longing to be understood, to be seen, to be listened to. It makes us feel connected. You demonstrate maturity when you can delay your own desire to be understood until you are clear about the other person's thoughts, feelings, and goals.

How do you ensure that you understand the other person?

- ✤ Ask questions
- ✤ Listen well to the answers
- ✤ Check your understanding for accuracy with the speaker
- ✤ Stay with the conversation until you both agree that you know what the other person intended to convey

There is a big difference between a *communication*—which is simply a message—and *communicating* which means the message has been received in the way it was intended!

Be Clear About What You Think And Want

Often, folks go into a difficult conversation focused on how they want the other person to change. Unless you are the boss with the clout to fire, that approach will likely backfire.

The only person's behavior you can change is your own. When entering a difficult conversation, take ownership of your part in the issue. In your preparation, look deeply into your own motives, words, and actions. *Be prepared to clarify your thinking and talk about your feelings.*

Invest Time In Preparation

When you have decided to embark on what you think might be a difficult conversation, do your homework first.

- ✦ What issue about the event concerns you?
- ✦ What would you like the outcome of the conversation to be?
- ✦ What feelings do you have about the issue?
- ✦ What is it about the issue that evokes those feelings?
- ✦ What would help you with the issue?
- ✦ What are you doing to maintain the issue? Aggravate it? Diminish it?
- ✦ What do you think is the best way to begin the conversation?
- ✦ What will you do to keep the conversation on a forward-moving track?
- ✦ What will you do if you derail?

Prepare. Prepare. Prepare.

Be Willing To Engage And Go The Extra Mile.

Be ready not only to understand the other person first, but to keep the conversation going until the difficulty is clarified, if not resolved. Know that it may well take more than one conversation.

Let the other person know that you appreciate their willingness to handle the issue. When progress has been made or a breakdown has occurred, step outside the issue.

Say something like,

> "I think that it might be best for us to take a break and re-visit this issue. Can we arrange a time now to meet again?"

Agreeing to continue the dialogue, until some process for managing the conflict is found, allows you to take the time—and the baby steps—you need to maintain safety and sanity.

Understand The Skills Required For Adequate Self-defense

Each person has the right to be treated respectfully. If you are feeling abused by the words of another, be sure to tell that person how you feel and how you would like to be spoken to . . . respectfully, of course.

It is perfectly reasonable to call a halt to a conversation in which you are repeatedly feeling abused. (If you find "abused" to be too strong, substitute "belittled", "put-down", "talked down to", "insulted", or . . .)

Understand The Difference Between Self-defense And Defensiveness

Self-defense is the act of defending yourself. NOTE: This is not the act of making excuses. It is simply the ability to speak up for yourself honestly and with integrity. It is stating your case without the need to make the other person wrong or blame them for your actions or feelings.

Defensiveness is an attempt to keep your opponent from scoring a point. It includes any tactic used to resist or prevent aggression. This includes the tit-for-tat kinds of conversation folks create in the guise of managing issues. You know the one:

> She: I wish you would refill the photocopier with paper if you use it all for your project.

He: Well, you're not always so perfect. What about leaving your coffee mugs in the sink?

That's defensiveness on his part. He is endeavoring to deflect the conversation from his behavior because it makes him uncomfortable and may require him to change.

Choose Appropriate Timing

Check with the other person to inquire if this is a good time to talk. If it is not a good time, ask to set a time for the difficult conversation. Before you even do that, make sure that you have chosen an optimum time to suggest, and that there will be sufficient time and a private space in which to converse.

Yes, you may have to bite your tongue just at the moment you would most like to speak. If you really want the relationship to move forward, though, choose your timing well to ensure the best result.

Remain Engaged

When words get tough, or hot, most folks have a tendency to run. Many folks take that one step further and want to both hit AND run! They want to have their say and stomp out without having to listen to the other. Sound familiar? Those conversations often take place at home, too.

Once you have met at the agreed upon time, you've done your homework, and you're feeling prepared, set some guidelines for the conversation. Discuss what you will do before emotions rise so you feel safer to proceed.

As I've said before, in any relationship the person who is most sane at the moment is responsible for the relationship. This particularly applies to difficult situations. *The first person to notice that the conversation has deteriorated from constructive to destructive can help the process by commenting on the change.* Check in to see if you both think it is a good time to quit and reschedule, or to continue the discussion.

Believe Peace Is Possible

The attitudes the parties bring to a difficult conversation determine the outcomes. When you approach a situation believing it can be remedied, you are ahead of the game.

Often, folks engage in negative self-talk:

"She'll never change."

"There's no point in even bringing it up."

"He's impossible."

. . . and much worse, right? If you believe that an agreement can be reached and demonstrate your willingness to engage in the process of finding it, you are part of the solution. If you refuse to discuss the issue, you remain part of the problem.

Which are you?

Knowing these things will not take the "difficult" out of difficult conversations. Few people seek out confrontation for enjoyment. Those who do may need more help than this book can offer! Call me for coaching.

When you do want to work something out with another person, following these guidelines will help you to bring your best to the table and therefore give your best to the conversation.

If it feels as though you must walk through minefields to reach your field of dreams, use these rules of engagement to ensure your safety and the safety of those around you. And . . . keep walking!

I cannot divine how it happens that the man who knows the least is the most argumentative.

Giovani della Casa

RHINO RAGE:

MANAGING ANGER: DON'T TELL ME TO CALM DOWN!

Growth in personality occurs as a consequence of meeting conflicts and impasses head on, and reconciling them. Interpersonal conflicts and impasses constitute problems which require solutions so that a satisfying relationship may be maintained. Whenever a person encounters a problem in his everyday living, he is obliged to vary his behavior until he discovers some mode of responding which is successful in achieving a solution.

Sidney Jourard

SMOOTHING RUFFLED FEATHERS

In the world of birds, ruffled feathers is one sign of a virus. Isn't that also the case at work? Ruffled feathers can spread like a virus throughout your office, department, or corporation. Depending on the influence of the ruffled one, that spread can be fatal.

Infected birds shed the virus by exhaling and excreting. Isn't this what happens in the workplace? Gossip and anger can quickly change the workplace environment from healthy to malicious—it's highly contagious.

When words are involved, a high level of refinement of the virus is possible. Stories change subtly. Emphasis is given to different aspects by different people. Additions are appended. Motives are questioned. Assumptions are made. Often, the initial event becomes entirely unrecognizable in a very short time.

What to do? Be H.I.P.!

||||||||||||||||||||||||||||||||||||||||||||||||||||||||||||||||||||||||||||||||||||||||||||||||||||||||||||||||||||||||||||||||||||||||||||||||||||

Here are three tips for smoothing ruffled feathers as soon as you notice them. Whether the ruffled or the ruffler, implement right way for best results.

BE HONEST

You may be thinking, "It was honesty that got me into this position in the first place!" True, you may have blurted out some unvarnished truth in a moment of frustration. That's often the fastest way to ruffle a few feathers.

Once you have calmed down some, it is time for a different kind of honesty. First, be honest with yourself.

- ✦ What was your intention when you opened your mouth?
- ✦ Did you intend to inflict pain?
- ✦ Did you intend to create tension and dissension?
- ✦ Did you really just want to smack the other person and end up doing it with your words?
- ✦ Or, were you just a little clumsy in trying to rectify a frustrating situation?

Now, if you are completely honest, it is likely that you so wanted rid of your frustration that you were lacking a little finesse. Right? If that is the case, you can now go to the person you ruffled and truthfully say that hurt was not your intent. Be honest about your outburst and identify it as a less than effective way of releasing your pain. Ask if you can discuss the issue and work out a solution that is acceptable to you both.

Oh, so, you really did want them to feel small, dumb, and inferior? In that case, you're on your own . . . likely looking for a new position. Of course, if you're the boss and you did this, you're also on your own . . . looking for new employees!

BE IMMEDIATE

Let no grass grow under your feet. **As soon as you have calmed down, or thought better of your words, go to the other person and acknowledge what's going on.** Take responsibility for your part in the interaction. Don't let this fester or spread.

Different people react differently to pain and stress. Some will internalize it and make themselves very uncomfortable, even unwell. Others will spread it around. This is the virus.

As soon as you can—as soon as your blood pressure is back to normal, your vision improves, and the blood has returned to your centers of reason and logic—**take responsibility for what you have done or said.** CAUTION: At this point, there is a tendency to degenerate into sentences involving the word *you*. Now is not the time for that. Speak only about *yourself* and *your* feelings. This takes practice.

Why be immediate? Because pain swells things. You've noticed that. You need to put ice on the situation right away. It's that simple.

BE POSITIVE

When folks are upset, there is a tendency to talk about what you don't want, won't put up with, and cannot stand any longer. Sure, that releases your frustration, however, it does not move the situation forward.

Talk about what you DO want, what WILL help, and what CAN smooth the way for a better working relationship. Be positive. Assuring folks that you want things to work is far better than screaming about what isn't working! You don't have to put on a Pollyanna approach to be positive. It is a simple flip of the mind-set. Switch from the past to the future.

"Let's do it this way!" is much easier to hear than
"I hate it when you ____!", isn't it?

Quick rule of thumb: Before you open your mouth, run the words you are about to say through your mind. Would you be able to hear it well? Will it help move the situation to resolution? If the answer is no, you've got time to change your words. If the answer is yes, then proceed with assurance that you are working to create the best consequences.

Any young duck can cruise through the pond knocking folks down. Smoothing ruffled feathers takes maturity, intelligence and willingness.

Don't be a dumb duck.
Learn to calm the waters and only create ripples that get you where
you want to go!

Rhoberta Shaler, PhD

Research shows that if unhealthy conflict goes unresolved for too long, team members are likely to leave the company or use valuable time to search for alternatives. Interestingly enough, this research applies to executive teams and implies that the role of the CEO in managing conflict at the executive level is crucial.

As reported in "How Commitment Affects Team Performance" by James Wallace Bishop & K. Dow Scott. Source: HR Magazine, Feb. 1997.

RHINO REALITY:
||||||||||||||||||||||||||||||||||||||||||||||||

RHINOS CHARGE AT EVERYTHING
THAT MOVES.

RULES FOR RECOGNIZING RHINOS:
||||||||||||||||||||||||||||||||||||||||||||||||||||||||||||||||||||||||||||||||||||||||

THEY ARE SO INSECURE, THEY FEEL MOST
POWERFUL WHEN THEY ARE RUNNING OTHER
PEOPLE OVER OR DOWN.

Anger ventilated often hurries toward forgiveness; anger concealed often hardens into revenge.

Edward Robert Bulwer-Lytton

WHAT DO YOU MEAN "I'M ANGRY"?

When you reach your boiling point, what do you do with the steam? Your choice at that moment makes all the difference in your relationships at home, at work, and with yourself.

Do you know when you are angry? Many folks don't. Not only are they unaware they're angry, but you would be surprised how few people actually understand their own behavior or how other folks see them, when in that frame of mind. They are not sensitive to their own attitudes, feelings, emotions, and communication style. This is a big problem . . . for everyone else.

Do you have high self-awareness? Do you have an accurate picture of your behavior, tone of voice, facial expressions? If you are unsure, sit down with the person you most trust and ask them to paint an honest picture for you. Yes, that may be difficult to ask, and to hear. It must be done, though, if you want to improve your relationships.

I recently heard a story about a manager whose employee presented a requested proposal for a new office system. After reading the proposal briefly, the manager went up one side of the employee and down the other.

She used language such as:

> "This is absurd."
> "What were you thinking?"
> "How long have you been with us?"
> "You're making me wonder why I ever hired you."

All this was delivered from a standing position in a loud voice with harsh eye contact. The employee, completely taken aback and intimidated, went back to her cubicle furious. Her colleague asked her about the meeting and she described the reception. Soon, the story made the rounds of the department.

The next week, the manager met a colleague who said to her,

> "Wow! You were really hard on Michelle. Are you planning on letting her go?"

The manager was stunned.

> "Why would you ever think that? She's important to our operation."

As they discussed the incident, the manager realized that she had no perception of the way she had delivered her blows to Michelle. She thought she had been simply responding to the ideas brought to her. She had no idea of the effect of her behavior on the employee. This manager needs to increase her self-awareness.

DO YOUR OWN WORK FIRST

What do you do when you're angry? How do you deliver your messages? Is your communication *clean*? Begin with yourself. How do you express your anger? *Do you* express your anger or does your steam escape in inappropriate ways at the wrong people, having been bottled up for too long? **Before you go telling others what they need to improve within themselves, look in the mirror.**

IMPROVE YOUR SKILLS

You likely have heard the old story about the husband who has been chewed out at work who comes home and yells at his wife who screams at the kids who kick the dog. If that husband had good communication and conflict management skills, he would have handled the issue at work in the first place.

If you feel intimidated, or you avoid conflict at all costs, you need skills. Take a community college course, participate in a teleseminar[1], and read some books. Seek out good ideas to increase your self-awareness and your skill set.

Conflict is not a four-letter word. It simply means to have divergent ideas, needs, drives, wishes, or demands. That's OK, but it is how we express those differences that takes the toll. **Learn to express differences in ways others will listen to. It will build your self-confidence.**

BEGIN SIMPLY

Pay attention to how you think, feel, and respond in different situations. Make a mental picture and rehearse how you would *like* to respond. Use your new skill set. Then, step out into the world.

Listen well when there is conflict. Look beneath the words to the pain. For example, when someone is angry with you because a piece of paper is missing, by listening carefully you may realize what is underneath the anger. You might then say,

> "I understand that not finding this piece of paper right now might make you late for your meeting, and you feel you may look inefficient."

Identify the real source of the pain. By giving it a name, both you and the other person deepen the understanding of the situation. When you get really good at this, you will also deepen your relationships. Taking the time to build your self-awareness and your skill set is well worth the effort.

Know anger when you see/feel it. Everyone in your life will benefit. You will benefit most of all.

---

1. You'll find descriptions & registration links for my teleseminars online at www.OptimizeInstitute.com

Thank God for EMOTION so that I can experience anger when appropriate and for a WILL to control my anger reaction as appropriate.

Tom Sheffler

ANGER IS HEALTHY

Anger is healthy. Anger is normal. It's how folks choose to express it that leads many astray. Anger is an arousal in your body caused by the perception of not having your needs met.

It is as dangerous and unsatisfying to internalize anger as it is to spread it around freely complete with expletives, loud voices, and threatening gestures. Both approaches to anger threaten relationships. One threatens the healthy relationship with yourself. Both threaten healthy relationships with others.

Anger is an indication of the perception of a boundary being crossed. Someone is doing something that you do not want done. It is also an indication of fear, frustration, or pain. Taking the time to articulate the reason for your anger is a great first step. Instead of screaming "I'm angry," take this important, gigantic step forward. Say,

> "I feel angry when _____ happens. I feel angry because it scares (frustrates or hurts) me."

Providing an insight into why you are experiencing the arousal of anger opens communication channels. Providing noise, movement, foul language, and sabre-rattling only causes others to want to fight, run, or freeze.

What are your current choices when you feel angry?
Think about your last week.

- ✦ When were you angry?
- ✦ Why were you angry?
- ✦ At whom were you angry?
- ✦ Did you express it?
- ✦ How did you express it?
- ✦ Did it move your relationship forward or push folks away from you?
- ✦ Did you turn it inward on yourself?

This can produce many physical symptoms that are unpleasant.

If anger is an issue for you, resolve to learn to manage it productively for all concerned.

RHINO REALITY:

RHINOS CHARGE AIMLESSLY AND UNPREDICTABLY.

RULES FOR RECOGNIZING RHINOS:

THEY ARE HAPPIEST WHEN THEY CAN KEEP THE OFFICE IN AN UPROAR.

**Remember not only to say the right
thing in the right place, but far more
difficult still, to leave unsaid the
wrong thing at the tempting moment.**

Benjamin Franklin

WHEN YOU SEE "RED" . . .

When you are feeling angry at someone, what do you do? Do you know how to express your feelings in ways that are clear and assertive? Many folks don't. For that reason, one of two things happens: they hold the anger in and, as we all know, it sneaks out in strange and often inappropriate ways; or they explode and scatter their unhappiness over everyone, perhaps destroying relationships on the way! Neither of these are healthy alternatives.

Anger is an arousal in the body that is triggered by frustration, fear, or hurt. As that arousal escalates, your body goes into the stress response. When that arousal raises your heart rate to about 120 to 150 beats per minute, the blood from the frontal lobes of your brain, the centers of reason and logic, drains down to protect your vital organs. This is not good news. Why? Because the more angry you become, the more unable you are to think clearly! You have probably experienced that. Just when you are at your loudest, wanting to deal the death blow to prove your righteous position, you cannot think. Then, you often say one of the best things you'll ever regret! Right?

When the body goes into arousal, **notice.**

If you are talking to someone at the time, *think.*

It is important to your well-being and the health of your relationships to answer this question:

> "What do you want as a result of this exchange?"

If a potentially volatile volley of words, accusations, and threats are likely to erupt, leave. No, this is not "running away from a fight". This is just informed decision-making.

There is one important difference, though: tell the person that you are leaving and when you will return to discuss the issue. This is the difference between being responsible and being a "hit-and-run" offender. Take care of the relationship by not abandoning the other person. Simply say,

> "I'm too angry now and I'm likely to say things I don't mean.
> I'll be back in three hours and let's discuss this then."

Why three hours or more? Simple. It takes ninety full minutes for the blood to return to your centers of reason and logic and your heart beat to return to normal, and sometimes, more!.

It makes good sense to wait and demonstrate that you care about yourself, the other person AND the relationship.

RHINO REALITY:

RHINOS ARE AMONG THE MOST AGGRESSIVE ANIMALS ALIVE TODAY.

RULES FOR RECOGNIZING RHINOS:

RHINOS FIGHT FOR OFFICES, THE BEST MUFFIN IN THE CAFETERIA, ATTENTION FROM THE BOSS, AND, SOMETIMES, JUST FOR THE SAKE OF IT.

**The most important single ingredient
in the formula of success is knowing
how to get along with people.**

Theodore Roosevelt

SO YOU CAN'T STAND THE PERSON IN THE NEXT OFFICE?

W hat to do? There is someone at work you really have difficulty liking. It may be mild or it may be on your mind long before you get to the office in the morning. It may cause you to consider staying home and giving up pay, just to avoid them. This can have a devastating effect on your day, not to mention on your career.

"Research shows that if unhealthy conflict goes unresolved for too long, team members are likely to leave the company or use valuable time to search for alternatives. Interestingly enough, this research applies to executive teams and implies that the role of the CEO in managing conflict at the executive level is crucial.[1]" So, you're in good company!

That information clearly demonstrates the need for pro-active communication and conflict management training, at all levels, in the workplace. Equip yourself with these skills. They will be endlessly useful in every area of your life.

When I work on these skills with corporate groups, the relief in the air is palpable. Simply put, folks feel a greater sense of self-confidence when they have the skills to confront difficulties. If your workplace is suffering, just one or two days of training can make an enormous difference. It makes sense.

Think of the lack of productivity that the stress of conflict creates. Who can attend to their work when they are concerned about possible confrontations, accusations, or cold shoulders? People have feelings. Feelings are powerful. **There is enough tension in the creativity and the deadlines that normal, productive work creates. Who needs tension caused by fear, poor communication and small minds?**

Work On Yourself First

The first and most important thing to do is to **examine your own behavior.** How are you treating that person you perceive as difficult? Is there anything in your posture, facial expression, or tone of voice that prevents friendly interaction? Often, when you have already decided that you don't like someone, or that they don't like you, that attitude is conveyed in your non-verbal communication. Work on yourself first.

Reach Out To Understand

Invite the other person out for lunch or coffee. This is a discovery time. Learn more about them. Are they having difficulties in their life outside the workplace? What interests them? What might you have in common that could move your relationship in a better direction? Spend this time learning.

When That Doesn't Work . . .

OK, so you have nothing in common. They were miserable and close-mouthed. Nothing good came from it. Good. You now know that you made the effort and can rest comfortably with that.

Next step, ask them for a meeting in the office. This takes courage, but how much courage is it currently taking just to show up every day? THIS IS NOT A "LET-ME-FIX-YOU" TYPE OF MEETING. Prepare for the meeting by creating a list of open-ended questions—ones that cannot be answered with a yes or no—that will hopefully create discussion between you such as:

> "How can we improve the relationship between us?"
> "What can we do to work together more collaboratively?"
> "Is there anything that I am doing that is causing this discomfort for you?"

Signify your willingness to create a workable relationship.

So, The Other Person Is Not Even Mildly Interested In Conversing About Change?

That is when you have a decision to make. Live with it, or take it to the next level. The next level involves bringing a third person into the conversation, a person who is willing to manage the situation because it is in the best interest of the workplace. A mediator may be offered. There may be other people on your team who are experiencing the same difficulties with the same person. This makes change more imperative for your superior. Point out the benefits of managing this issue to the company.

No matter how it seems, no one really likes conflict.

- Some people create it because it allows them to feel they have a modicum of control
- Others create it as a cover for how little they are doing
- Others have their own reasons and needs for keeping things in an uproar

You, though, always have a choice. You can always do something to remove the tension even if it means making a career shift. Sometimes, it's worth it, but only after you have done everything in your power to improve things.

**Remember, confrontation is not a four-letter word!
It simply means "a face-to-face meeting."**

1. James Wallace Bishop & K. Dow Scott, "How Commitment Affects Team Performance". *HR Magazine*, Feb. 1997.

**Just as the hand that strikes the
ground cannot fail, so is the ruin
certain of him who cherishes anger.**

Tiruvalluvar (c. 5th century A.D.),

I JUST DON'T KNOW WHY HE GETS UNDER MY SKIN!

Have you ever been "gone around" at work? You know those times when you are the point person for a particular project and your requests for cooperation are ignored or you feel purposefully left out of the loop. I was coaching a management team once where this was common. No wonder they were at each others' throats!

Whatever could be the purpose of agreeing on lines of communication or on division of roles and responsibilities and then not following them? Well, that's simple. There are people who think they will be noticed, valued, or recognized for their initiative by doing this. They are mistaken. There are other people who think the rules do not apply to them. They, too, are mistaken. We have all seen cases, however, where—unfair as it truly is—this ploy has worked! That is a whole other topic!

And, there are still other people who behave in a different way. These folks promise to do a task or follow agreed-upon guidelines and then repeatedly fail to perform. These are the folks who get under our skin, right?

As I was interviewing each member of that management team, I learned there was one person of the eight who regularly circumvented the lines of communication, client assignment, AND courtesy. In each reported instance, this fellow, when challenged, came up with weak reasons for his behavior. Each one was couched in his desire to not inconvenience his co-worker, or his intention to "take something off their plate," or simply "I forgot." This is insidious. If it had happened only one time and the colleague had clearly re-stated their agreements, that would have been one thing. But it happened repeatedly with more than one colleague. It was a habit.

There are four main categories into which we can place behavior: passive, aggressive, assertive, or, passive-aggressive.

Assertive behavior is the most productive although there are times when aggressive or passive behavior is a necessary choice.

Which style is the fellow above demonstrating? Likely, passive-aggressive—which may be the most infuriatingly deceptive behavior on the planet!

Peggy Elam, a past president of the Nashville Area Psychological Association, offers these insights:

> "Passive-aggressive behaviors are those in which negative emotions—especially anger—are expressed indirectly through negative attitudes and resistance to reasonable requests. For instance, a worker resentful of another employee's accomplishments may be consistently late or disruptive in meetings or settings in which his or her co-worker is lauded.
>
> An employee angry at the boss for a last-minute assignment may purposefully botch the task in some way rather than directly telling the boss there isn't enough time to do it properly. Passive-aggressive behaviors are fairly common, especially when people feel powerless to assert their desires directly . . . passive-aggressive individuals

express their resistance to others—especially in work settings—by 'procrastination, forgetfulness, stubbornness, and intentional inefficiency, especially in response to tasks assigned by authority figures.' They feel unappreciated and misunderstood, and they constantly complain to those around them. They blame difficulties on others and may be sullen, irritable, impatient, argumentative and cynical. They often focus their discontent (and resistance) toward authority figures, which can include not only bosses but also parents, teachers or spouses who take a parental role."[1]

It is the gradual and cumulative effect of working with passive-aggressive people that eventually takes its toll on a work group or team. So, what do to?

If such a person has found his or her way into your workplace, it is time to take action. Of course, if this is the boss we're speaking of, that action may be taking a hike. Let's consider your options for managing this behavior in co-workers.

E-MAIL IS YOUR ALLY!

Make it a practice to take one minute after any meeting—whether just two of you or the entire team—to clarify by e-mail the results and agreements made. Have each attendee sign-off on this by simply replying. Do this even when you think it is unnecessary. Great! One giant step to removing any lack of clarity.

ESTABLISH GUIDELINES FOR MANAGING DEADLINES

It is always wise for any team to step aside from task-oriented issues and establish process guidelines. Decide what the procedure will be if anyone can see that they cannot complete their undertakings in a timely manner. This might be an agreement that, if a task cannot be done in time, that information needs to be communicated to the group at least two days prior to the deadline. This leaves time for others to adjust, resources to be found, or the deadline to be moved. It's your decision. Having these agreements again leads to clarity.

ESTABLISH PROCESS FOR DISCUSSING IDEAS AND CHALLENGES

Your workplace or work team is much more effective, cohesive, and productive when issues can be discussed openly. Trust is completely eroded when people gossip. Wipe this out!

Create process in your meetings where challenges can be brought forward to the group. This is not the blame game. It is a systems approach. Is there something in our process that is consistently creating a hold-up? If that something is *someone*, ask for his or her cooperation. Help to define the challenges. Describe the behavior and describe its effect on team outcomes. Do this in a very neutral way.

If you have a passive-aggressive person on your team, implement the steps above. Unfortunately, few of these folks satisfactorily change quickly. Their issues stem from childhood and can seldom be changed on the job. Of course, with enough time, trust, and attention, it is possible for them to believe that they are valued, have value, and are safe. Once they feel appreciated and understood, they can give up their constant complaints and excuses. They can also begin to accept that they are the author of their behaviors rather than blaming difficulties on others. If their skills are of great value to your workplace, you will particularly want to take immediate action on the steps above.

Perhaps you are not in a position to implement these steps. The co-worker may simply be someone you sit next to all day. That is the time for your personal boundaries to be given a voice. **Remember, it is always your responsibility to teach people how to treat you. Speak up!**

Establish plans and processes for managing conflicts, confrontations, and expectations. Manage passive-aggressive behavior proactively to avoid wide-spread dis-ease.

1. Peggy Elam. Passive-Aggressive. Article on Emotional Health found online at www.ivillagehealth.com

RHINO REALITY:
||||||||||||||||||||||||||||||||||||||||||||||

RHINOS ARE VERY AGILE AND CAN TURN QUICKLY IN A SMALL SPACE.

RULES FOR RECOGNIZING RHINOS:
||||||||||||||||||||||||||||||||||||||||||||||||||||||||||||||||||||||||||||||||||||||||

THEY HAVE A TENDENCY TO BE PASSIVE-AGGRESSIVE AND CAN TURN YOUR WORDS AROUND ON A DIME.

**I have never been hurt by anything I
didn't say.**

Calvin Coolidge

MALPRACTICE OF THE MOUTH

I s your mind your greatest asset? Do you suffer from malpractice of the mouth? That is the malady that occurs when the mouth enrages before the mind engages! BEWARE: You may work with someone afflicted!

There is no room in the workplace for verbal violence. None! *It is inappropriate, unacceptable, and definitely unprofessional.* No allowances for verbal violence should be made for educated and mentally competent adults in positions of authority. NONE!

Folks who yell and curse (and some who add obscenities) are using their words in the same way they would use their fists—it is no more sophisticated. It is both a sign of lack of skills and a symptom of unmanaged frustration. They need help—help to express their feelings and their need for control appropriately.

Should providing this help be the responsibility of the organization? That is an important question. Employees who are doing an excellent job in most areas are the consideration. They are valuable AND they have a people skills gap. The good news is that people skills can be taught. The bad news is that some folks do not want to learn them. So, the first assessment that must be made is the willingness of the employee to examine and improve their skills. No number of training hours can *make* a person change.

A few years ago, I was delivering a program on managing difficult people successfully. As this is a program I often delivered, some agencies regularly sent folks to it. One woman appeared in the course three times in three years. At one break, she complained to me,

> "I just don't know why they keep sending me on this silly course. I know it by heart. It's a waste of their money."

Well, I knew why she was there. She was the "difficult person" and she just would not internalize the information being given to her. You know, we may all be someone else's idea of a difficult person at times. This woman was the poster child. She was bright enough. She was able to grasp the concepts, but she simply would not apply them to herself. Perhaps, she is still being sent to courses like that . . . and still complaining about it!

Confrontation is not a four letter word. Neither should it employ certain four letter words.

A confrontation adds the dynamic of differing opinions to a conversation. It is possible to have a conversational confrontation when folks have skills and willingness to actually communicate.

Verbal violence is most often a scream for attention, a misguided demand for respect, or an attempt to exert control. All three come from fear. Certainly you can understand those fears, however, two things must happen to make the workplace safe:

- ✦ The violator must change his or her ways
- ✦ The violated must express his or her boundaries

Verbal violence is clearly harassment. It has no place in the workplace. Yes, every now and then, mistakes are made—tempers flare and apologies are accepted. That goes with the territory of being human. It is when verbal violence is a management style that steps must be taken. Whether you are managing other folks or managing your personal life, violence leads to alienation, the very thing the violator is seeking most to avoid!

FIRST THINGS, FIRST.

IF YOU ARE THE VIOLATOR . . .

Stop! Step away and reflect on your needs for attention, respect, and control. Are those needs healthy? Are they serving you well? Are they appropriate in this circumstance? If not, find help.

IF YOU ARE THE VIOLATED . . .

Remember, anytime that you take the bait and participate in a verbal violence loop with someone, you are letting them get away with inappropriate and abusive behavior. Anytime you cower and retreat, you are also letting them get away with it.

Simply say that you find their treatment of you unacceptable and that you are willing to have a conversation when it can be done with respectful dialogue—and then move away.

Also, tell the violator that if change does not occur your next step is to inform a higher authority of the verbal violence, the harassment. Then do it.

Yes, I know that sounds simple and it is not always easy. Putting up with anger in any form is not easy, either!

Remember, you are responsible for teaching people how to treat you . . . everywhere.

Verbal violence will not stop until you take the actions necessary to stop it! Just do it!

**I like people who refuse to speak until
they are ready to speak.**

Lillian Hellman

ZIP IT!!

If your first impulse is to speak up when you see or feel something is wrong in your workplace, zip it! Yes, just zip it! Why? Most folks' initial responses are impulsive, emotional, subjective, and void of thought.

That old count-to-ten rule isn't a bad idea at all. A *Ninety-Minute Rule* is an even better one. Why? Well, there are two good reasons.

> **#1 You may not have all the facts or the big picture.** Taking a step back from the situation will give you a better perspective and your perception may change.

> **#2 Give your brain a chance to recover.** If the situation angered you, ninety minutes will allow the blood to return to your brain's centers of logic.

When anyone gets angry, blood rushes away from the brain to the vital organs. That is nature's way of ensuring survival. Unfortunately, when the blood leaves the brain, your rational, logical thought also leaves. And that is the worst time to engage your mouth. Many folks have made the best speech they will ever regret when they are the most angry. Can you relate to that?

It takes most folks a full ninety minutes to recover from full-blown anger. Why chance it? Even if you were just a little bit angry, give yourself enough time to be able to form full, coherent sentences!

Obviously, there are times when you simply must take control of a crisis. Knowing now that you may not be at your best at that moment, speak only as much as damage control requires.

Refrain from being sarcastic, judgmental, or rude. Simply do as little as you can while managing the situation. Then retreat.

The more you exercise control over your negative outbursts and knee-jerk reactions to people or issues, the more you present yourself as mature and controlled. Oh yes, and you'll spend far less time making apologies, too.

Just zip it until you're sure it's safe to open your mouth!

WHAT TO DO FIRST WHEN FEAR HITS YOUR WORKPLACE

You hear that layoffs are coming. Someone is called to the supervisor's office. Word travels through the workplace. Fear creeps in. It is said that, in times of drought, the animals down at the watering hole look at each other differently[1]. Are folks looking at each other differently at your water cooler?

Your body has a mind of its own. When it senses fear, it immediately goes into a protective mode. Your shoulders move towards your earlobes. Your digestion slows down. You become hyper-vigilant. Your hands and feet become cold as the blood rushes to protect vital organs (leaving your brain all alone). In fact, the blood first leaves the frontal lobes whose job is associated with reasoning, planning, parts of speech, movement, emotions, and problem solving. Great! Just what you need is the first to go!

Knowing this, then, it is imperative that you keep your head about you in tense times. Easy to say! *Fortunately, not so difficult to do.* Here are some suggestions—no, really, imperatives—for triumphing in tense times.[2]

BE POSITIVELY SELFISH

Take very good care of yourself. This is important at all times, however, it is *essential* in tense times. Do these five things every day, without fail:

1. **Breathe deeply in through your nose and exhale slowly through your mouth five times.** Do this often throughout your day. This is the best mini-vacation on the planet. You'll notice that your shoulders naturally relax as you exhale through your mouth. The increase of oxygen to your brain is also appreciated.

2. **Go for a walk for at least thirty minutes each day.** Breathe well and relax your body. This is a time to enjoy the beauty that you see. If you are walking in nature, see it there. If you are walking on a city street, see it in the people you meet. *Find it.* If your mind begins to race, do #1 above and re-focus on what you are seeing.

3. **Put your personal affairs in order.** Clean your office, your space, your home, your closets. Doing things over which you have control is calming. Take back overdue library books. Pay fines. Return borrowed items. Write that letter you've been putting off. Make a will. Organize your finances.

4. **Focus on your goals.** What do you want to have accomplished one week, month, or year from now? What are your plans for achieving these goals? What can you do pro-actively right now to move forward? *Again, take control of what is in your control.* This is important.

5. **Eat nutritious foods.** You know this and your mind will play tricks when you are tense. What you think of as comfort foods may be just the things that increase your discomfort. Sugars, for instance, seem comforting, however, they can contribute to a feeling of depression. Many folks think that coffee keeps them going when things are tough. It may give them that illusion. Coffee is not only a stimulant but also a diuretic. That means it is taking vital water from your cells just when you need it most. It creates tension . . . and the desire for another cup!

BE ATTENTIVE

It is easy to become hyper-vigilant when fearful in the workplace. This is a natural response to high-stress or trauma. Once one challenge has happened, there is a heightened expectation of more to follow. So, be attentive and avoid responding to hyper-vigilance.

How do you do this? When something happens that could be construed as an indication of a problem, say, you see two colleagues chatting quietly together, ask yourself a few questions:

✤ If lay-offs were not an issue, would this behavior seem problematic?

✤ Am I labeling or judging this behavior inappropriately?

✤ How am I intensifying the fear by my reactions and behaviors?

✤ Am I doing anything that might be causing others discomfort?

This will help you adjust your perspective to maintain balance.

Be attentive to your own behavior. When you focus on what you can contribute rather than what you fear, several benefits follow:

✤ You are calmer.

✤ You help others feel more settled.

✤ Your focus makes you more valuable in the workplace.

✤ You become a leader.

BE PRO-ACTIVE

Keep your head up out of the sand. Be aware of the realities of your current situation and plan for them realistically. If your first reaction is panic, set aside an hour to just worry. Get it out of your system. Worry really well and use that hour fully. Then, look for actual evidence in reality of the best plan for yourself.

✤ Read magazines and reports from your industry.

✤ What are the trends?

✤ What are the needs?

✦ Do you need more training?

✦ Is re-location an option?

This would be a good time to assess your goals and focus on your next steps.

✦ Talk with others in your field, preferably, those in charge.

✦ Ask your questions.

✦ Clarify the intentions of the organization.

✦ Ask how and if your position is likely to be affected.

✦ Don't wait to be a result. Be a cause!

Your life is too important to live in fear in your workplace. You have goals. You have skills. You have direction. You have a voice. Take charge of fear. You know that you are the only person who is responsible for your responses to life. Choose responses that support you.

Too many people fail to step up to the plate in their own game of life. Step up! Be positively selfish[3], attentive, and pro-active.

1. For more on this, see the last chapter, "When the Watering Hole Shrinks"
2. Want to triumph in tense times? Get Dr. Shaler's e-book, *Pack Your Own Parachute: Top Ten Tactics for Taming Tense Times*. It's got many other ideas and strategies. Also available in print in bulk for company-wide distribution. www.OptimizeInstitute.com.
3. Get Dr. Shaler's audio program, *Creating Your Life*, for more tips on being positively selfish.

RHINO REALITY:
||||||||||||||||||||||||||||||||||||||||||||||

RHINOS ARE EXTREMELY TERRITORIAL.

RULES FOR RECOGNIZING RHINOS:
||||||||||||||||||||||||||||||||||||||||||||||||||||||||||||||||||||||||||||||||||||||

RHINOS ARE DEFINITELY NOT TEAM-PLAYERS.

**Fear defeats more people than any
other one thing in the world.**

Ralph Waldo Emerson

BACKSTABBERS LOSE

Whatever are people thinking when they are two-faced? Are they really thinking that people are stupid and can't see the forest for the trees?

When meetings take place surreptitiously, behind closed doors and blinds, suspicion builds. I was working with a finance department for a major agency. The director was well-known—and feared—for her supposed open door policy. Loudly she proclaimed that anyone at any time was welcome to come and speak with her in her office. She declared that she wanted open communication and that everyone should feel able to talk with her. Sounds great. So, what was the problem?

When a brave person would muster up his or her courage and take the director at her word, it was likely that, within moments, the yelling voice of the director could be heard throughout the department, complete with language suitable for a gutter! Oh, but that was not all! Seconds later, the door of her office would slam shut and the blinds would snap—the once hopeful employee trapped inside—and the abuse would continue.

When I was brought in as consultant, trainer, and coach, my task was to create a functioning team from these nine people: one screamer, three middle managers living on tenterhooks, and five subordinates afraid to speak or step sideways. Whew! You can believe that there were many days that those folks seriously considered sick leave!

People enjoy power. Some people abuse power. And, they do it from fear. No one needs to abuse power when they feel secure, when they know they are competent and capable, when they have nothing to prove.

Some people feel they have to stomp on and mess with folks in order to get a promotion. In some dysfunctional businesses, this is true. I was working with an executive coaching client whose boss wanted harmony at any price. The boss was petrified of managing conflict in his office. My client was bringing in great clients (and their money), but her subordinate did not like her. The boss, in his wisdom, decided to release my client rather than deal with the underhanded and in-her-face behavior of the subordinate. All in the name of peace. Strange things happen in the corporate world sometimes.

Of course, the opposite could also happen. The person who brings in the most money could be allowed to trample over the subordinates because the bottom line is more important than respect.

A reader wrote to me about a director who plays power games. This woman calls meetings at inconvenient times and invites her favorites along. This requires people to shift priorities, upset family plans, and give up weekends just to satisfy this woman's whims. But, she takes the abuse of power to a whole new level. Once everyone has changed their plans to accommodate her, she changes her mind, changes the meeting time, and the shifting begins again. What an incredibly insecure woman!

Backstabbing, gossiping, greed, and power games are a sign of an unhealthy organization. Worse though, those who engage in such things are wasting vital energy and making themselves miserable.

You might think that eliminating the game-playing and control-brokering will eliminate you from the promotion ranks. You might think that you don't know well enough how the game is played. Ask yourself this question:

"Am I willing to give up my integrity and peace of mind on a daily basis in order to play into someone else's misguided power games?"

What is the real prize?

Yes, I know, you need the pay check. We all do need to be able to earn our keep. How about this, though? How about you behave in integrity with your values and refuse to play? Wouldn't that feel better? Would you enjoy each day more? Eventually, folks will get the message.

BE THE APPRECIATOR

Mention the things you appreciate. Comment on the things you like. Discuss what you prefer.

William James, the father of psychology, said,

> "The deepest craving of the human nature is the need to be appreciated."

Appreciation is cost-free. Move the things you like forward by talking about them. It takes almost no effort to find something you appreciate about each person you know. Just give voice to it. Guess what? You'll be appreciated.

NEVER SAY ANYTHING YOU DON'T WANT TO BE TRUE

Wow! This one can change the face of the planet, let alone the culture of your workplace. **Speak about what you want to see happen, what would improve things. Focus on the positive and give voice to it.**

I'll say it again. This is not Pollyanna thinking. It's why I wrote the book, *What You Pay Attention to Expands*—because it's true. How much energy do you lose when you engage in the "poor me" and "ain't-it-awful" conversations? You're doing it to yourself.

I'll bet you would not list gossip, backstabbing, or negativity as any of the desirable values you hold dear. But, are you behaving as though that were true? Remember, your behavior is your belief and there is no way around that one!

BE PRO-ACTIVE

First rule of change:
Be the change you want to see in the world.

That's what Mahatma Gandhi said and I believe it is paramount. How many people expect behaviors from others that they are not demonstrating themselves?

- ⟡ Talk about what you want to create
- ⟡ Keep the buzz going about what is possible
- ⟡ Influence the culture of your workplace with your presence
- ⟡ Be strong
- ⟡ Be the voice for fair play and reason

Would that person who calls those meetings that inconvenience everyone be happy if it happened to her? No, she would be the first to complain.

Would the person who runs to you with the latest gossip be thrilled to be the topic of conversation tomorrow morning? No, he would be outraged and declare it unfair.

Would the backstabber cry when stabbed? Louder than anyone.

Stop this nonsense. Just stop it. **Refuse to play.** It will soon end the game and, if not the whole game, it will end the game around you.

I'm not talking about being a wuss, a doormat, or a snob. This is about being in integrity with what you value, with being the person you most want to be. Use your energy, time, and resources in ways that make you feel good every day. After all, it is *your* quality of life you're creating!

There are risks. You may be happier. People may gravitate towards you and want to play on your team. You may become a leader and have the opportunity to demonstrate a better way of doing things.

Of course, there are other risks. You may be seen as different and no fun at all. Some folks don't like people to rain on their pity parties! Or, you may catch the eye of the offender in power. Guess what? You'll be the one who is promulgating positivity. You'll be the one showing that there is another (and better) way to make it through the work day. And, they just may want you on their team. Why? Because you are easy to be around.

OK, now do the math. You're easy to be around while sharing what's possible for the team, department or company. That has to be attractive. Hang in.

Backstabbers lose every day. Not only will you be winning every day personally, you very well may win the day.

Be a shift shaper!

**Make no friends with those given
to anger, and do not associate with
hotheads, or you may learn their ways
and entagle yourself in a snare.**

The Bible: Hebrew Proverbs 22:24-25

RHINO REALITY:
IIIIIIIIIIIIIIIIIIIIIIIIIIIIIIIIIIIIIIIIIII

RHINOS INTERBREED.

RULES FOR RECOGNIZING RHINOS:
IIIIIIIIIIIIIIIIIIIIIIIIIIIIIIIIIIIIIIIIIIIIIIIIIIIIIIIIIIIIIIIIIIIIIIIIIIIIIIII

**WORKING (OR LIVING) WITH A RHINO CAN GIVE
YOU A VERY THICK HIDE. BEWARE: WHEN TWO
OR MORE GET TOGETHER, THERE IS GOING TO
BE TROUBLE.**

**Reprove thy friend privately, commend
him publicly.**

Solon

RHINO WRANGLING:

NEGOTIATING SKILLS THAT GET YOU WHAT YOU WANT

**Make thyself a craftsman in speech,
for thereby thou shalt gain the upper
hand.**

Ancient Egyptian Tomb Inscription

NEGOTIATING IS
THE WAY OF LIFE

You negotiate all day long. If you are not doing it with yourself, you're doing it with others. Nothing could be simpler or broader in scope than negotiation. Every need that you want met is a potential negotiation. Sometimes subtle, sometimes overt—negotiating happens continuously.

And, it all depends on your desire and ability to communicate. Negotiating expert Gerard Nierenberg[1] says that *"negotiation occurs when human beings exchange ideas for the purpose of changing their relationships."* Now do you believe that you really are negotiating all day?

In my work as a mediator and negotiator, I know the value and importance of every negotiated solution satisfying some of the needs of both parties. Although it sometimes appears that one side is a clear winner and the other a loser, those situations seldom stay settled. I'll bet that has been your experience. Every solution must have a win in it for all concerned. Why? Because life goes on. The story doesn't end after the negotiation. Those who feel as though they lost completely will eventually want something from the winner and the animosity will carry through and erupt again in all likelihood.

So, how are your negotiation skills? Would you rather ride sixty miles bareback on an old mule than negotiate? Many folks behave as though they would.

NEGOTIATION REQUIRES SELF-ESTEEM

You have to have some self-esteem to negotiate. You have to believe that your point, your desire, or your concern is worthy of resolution. In my therapy and coaching practice, I've seen folks who are hurting badly in personal relationships or in the workplace who will not speak up. It takes two people to negotiate.

If you don't bring up your issue, you are foolish to think you will ever be free of the frustration, hurt, or fear related to it. The other party is obviously getting what they want in your silence. While you are being a doormat, they are cleaning their shoes on you. It's unlikely they are going to bring it up, right?

When the pain, hurt, and frustration—the basic emotions that cause the arousal in the body known as anger—are too much to bear, people with low self-esteem quit their jobs, leave their relationships, and slip away. That's one tactic. Unfortunately, folks who do that often get a lot of mileage through telling their "ain't it awful, s/he done me wrong" stories repeatedly.

Guess what? Every time they re-tell the story they re-live the pain on the cellular level . . . and they stay angry! They may even use it as an excuse for their behavior now. Many people do that with stories from the past, even from their childhoods when they were not able to negotiate. It's hard to negotiate with an adult when you're seven years old!

You need healthy self-esteem to negotiate. **You need to believe you deserve to be treated well and to ask for what you want. You may not always get it but you are entitled to ask.**

NEGOTIATION REQUIRES PREPARATION

Anger is not preparation for negotiation. Never negotiate when you are angry. Your ability to reason diminishes as your anger increases.

Preparation entails knowing what you want and why you want it, AND understanding the world from the other person's point of view. Logically examine why the other person may be behaving in the ways that you want changed, or why they want what they want from you. Remember, I said *logically.* When your emotions start to rise, take a few deep breaths and come back when you can think clearly.

Remember, "Negotiation is an exchange of ideas for the purpose of changing the relationship."

You had better be clear about which ideas you want to exchange. And, no expletives can help!

Know what outcome would be satisfying to you. Know your absolute best outcome as well as what you could live with as an alternative to getting it all your way. Remember, you are looking for a *solution that satisfies both parties* so that the matter can end right here. You don't want to be back at the table, still furious, next week . . . or even next year!

NEGOTIATION REQUIRES FLEXIBILITY

We negotiate problems, not demands. Demands carry with them so much emotional charge that anger ensues. Remember how the body works. The angrier you get, the less blood gets to your brain and the more brain-dead you become. Opening your mouth then is extremely hazardous to your well-being! When we come to negotiation with an open mind, we may learn something. This is a good thing.

Many folks have made assumptions about the people and situations that bother them. Understanding your own assumptions and the assumptions the other party may have made is wise. You may be taking things personally that have little or nothing to do with you, too.

A couple went into a roadhouse for lunch. The waitress was slamming things on the table, sighing, and making every request the couple made seem like an unreasonable demand that she should not have to deal with.

The two were shocked. They were thinking:

> "What kind of service was this? What kind of place was this to have such a surly waitress? There'll be no tip for her. This is absolutely unacceptable. How dare she?"

The assumption was that the couple were not worthy of better service or greater respect. They took it personally.

After a few minutes, another waitress approached the table and said in a quiet voice,

> "Excuse your waitress. She's usually a million laughs but she's having a very difficult time. Her husband walked out yesterday and left her with four kids, no money, and huge debts. Please understand."

Ooh. Different story. The couple's assumptions were wrong. The poor service had nothing to do with them or the restaurant. It was a situation that could use a little understanding. Sure, it would have been best if the waitress had been able to keep her problems away from the table. But, the couple decided to respond to her with kindness. Their attitude changed. True, they could not get all that they wanted from the situation but their perspective had shifted. They even tipped well.

Flexibility is an essential quality to exercise in your life. Rigidity causes things to break.

Negotiation skills can be learned. When I'm giving my seminar, "How to Negotiate Anything with Anyone at Any Time[2]," people are surprised to learn that they are indeed negotiating much of the day. Why not learn the skills that make it easiest on all concerned?

Sure, you'll run into some immovable objects in your lifetime. That's a given. You will, however, know that you were able to pose your questions, put forward your views and ask for what you need and want with competence.

Doormats get discarded once they are too dirty and worn. They are replaced. Don't be one! Learn to negotiate well.

1. Gerald I. Nierenberg. *The Complete Negotiator.* (Barnes & Noble Books, 1986.)
2. Dr. Shaler offers both introductory and advanced negotiation seminars. *Teleseminars for individuals and teams are also available.* All information can be found at www.OptimizeInstitute.com

ASSERTING YOURSELF UNDER PRESSURE

When things heat up or an interaction is critical, you need strong skills that you can depend on. When emotions rise, stress is created. When we are most stressed, our abilities of reason of logic leave us stranded, often tongue-tied or stammering. This is not necessary.

In much the same way you learned to drive your car, you acquire competent, confident, and comfortable communication, conflict, anger, and negotiation skills. On those first days behind the wheel, you might have asked yourself:

⊕ What do I push?

> **The basic difference between being assertive and being aggressive is how our words and behavior affect the rights and well being of others.**
>
> Sharon Anthony Bower

- ⊕ When do I push?
- ⊕ Why?
- ⊕ All at once?
- ⊕ What do I need to know?
- ⊕ What do I pay most attention to?
- ⊕ What will happen if I don't?
- ⊕ Where do I look?
- ⊕ How can I make this all work together?
- ⊕ How do I coordinate my eyes, brain, ears, hands & feet?
- ⊕ Do I look in the rearview mirror?
- ⊕ Do I concentrate on the windshield view?

It's the same with learning new ways to proceed with positive communication and negotiation. You are doing multiple things at once, paying attention on many levels, while moving in the direction of your goals. For a while, it all seems too much to remember . . . and especially when you are somewhat brain-impaired from heightened emotional arousal! Keep going. All you need is effective skills and constant practice. Just like driving.

Following are clear skills and strategies to:

- ⊕ Assert yourself
- ⊕ Keep your blood pressure lowered
- ⊕ Achieve your desired outcomes
- ⊕ Feel more comfortable, competent and confident

ESSENTIAL ELEMENTS FOR ASSERTING YOURSELF

Acknowledge the feelings, efforts, predicaments, or motives of the other person

This is key. It forces you to look beyond yourself and observe what is going on with the other person. It takes you out of yourself and your feelings to recognize it is not only about you. Just at the moment you most want to be seen, you learn to switch your focus away from yourself.

"I can see/hear that you are frustrated . . . "
"You have said that you're anxious to settle this . . . "
"I have heard about the stress that you are carrying . . . "

Take the time to acknowledge what you have seen, felt, learned, heard, or gathered. Even if you are not correct, you will open the conversation to further clarification.

Commit involvement on your part

Before you ever get into the specific issues, let the other person know that you are committed to working things out. A major fear of any person who is feeling hurt, frustrated, scared, or piqued is that they are going to be abandoned either physically or emotionally. Offer assurance that you are interested and willing to stay with the process.

"I'd like to settle this with you."
"I'm going to talk with you about ways we can turn this corner and . . . "
"I want to handle this issue well and I would like to make an appointment with you."

Even though you may have some trepidation about the actual conversation, it is good to know *when* it will be discussed. It gives you time to prepare and to collect your thoughts. It is reassuring to know that there is sufficient commitment to the relationship to want to shift confrontation to communication.

Take the time you need

Whenever you can give information that allows another person to understand that you value the relationship and know its importance, do so. Focus on the needs of the conversation.

"We need to go slowly. This is too important to rush."

and, mean it!

If the relationship, whether business or personal, is worth keeping, it is definitely worth taking the time to understand each other well. Even though it may *seem* unnecessary to mention, this clearly indicates that the relationship has value.

Describe behavior in terms of the senses

One big problem most folks have when they enter a discussion of importance that has a high emotional charge is they ascribe meaning to the other person's behavior. BEWARE! You are much safer describing what you see and hear than you are deciding what it means. They'll tell you, believe me.

> "When I see your face red, your eyes bulging and your breath coming in short burst, I wonder . . . "

It's not rocket science. Slowing down the communication when it really counts can make all the difference!

Notice and name any discrepancies when you hear or feel them

Sometimes, we think we understand. Sometimes, we assume we are right. Both are dangerous. Demonstrate that you are listening well by asking questions when things do not add up for you. By owning your own confusion, you are not making the other person wrong. You are simply looking to understand more fully.

> "I'm confused. On one hand, you say ____ and yet you ____. Please help me to understand."

Can you see how this level of positive verbal communication can encourage another person to open up? To feel safe? You must do this with the best of intentions, and a true curiosity to understand. Any attempts to be manipulative will damage the relationship, often irreparably.

Stop and summarize

Whenever you feel at an impasse, or are unsure of where to go next in a conversation, stop and summarize. Step outside the conversation and say,

> "I think we have made progress ____ and ____. I believe I understand that you feel/want/need/expect _____. Have I got it right?"

This gives both of you a break, releases tension, and allows for further clarification.

Give your partner a "weather report"

This is a very important step. You simply let the other person know the effect of their behavior on you. You may be completely surprised by how another person interprets and is affected by your behavior. Offer a look into your lens.

> "I get defensive when . . . "
> "I can't listen well when . . . "
> "I get completely stuck and don't know where to go when . . ."

It is a good idea to let the other person know that you are human, too.

Make no assumptions . . . but, if you do, label it as such

Assumptions about another's thoughts, feelings, or motives can lead to big trouble. It is much simpler to ask than it is to assume. If, however, you have made an assumption, label it as such.

> "I assume that this means _____"
> "I have a hunch that where this is going is _____"

Do not state your assumptions as facts. That creates an unnecessary layer of confusion or controversy. *At any time* it is much wiser to ask questions than make statements!

Ask probing questions to increase your understanding

Many times, in a effort to shorten a conversation or get to a quick fix, little time is taken to learn. This is definitely counter-productive. Take the time to ask questions that will solicit further information from the other person.

> "I'd like to find out what it is about _____"
> "I would like to know more about how you arrived at that _____"

Probe for the intention beneath any statement as well. Take the time. It will shorten the process and strengthen the relationship.

Clarify your intent

Don't make the other person guess what you are up to. It erodes trust. Just tell them.

> "It's not my intent to _____"
> "I'd like to work towards _____(solution)."

Again, it's not rocket science! Be up-front. Honesty is still the best policy.

Offer some agreement

You may not agree with everything the other person says, but you can usually find some point from which you share the view. This is an especially good strategy when you are receiving criticism with which you disagree.

You can *agree in part* which will dispel statements that are intended as a put-down:

> A: "You're always at work. You don't care about your family."
> B: "Yes, I do work a lot."

That deflected the sting and allowed the conversation to continue.

You can *agree in probability* when there is some chance that your critic is correct:

> "You could be right." (This is my personal favorite of all time!!!)
> "It may be that . . . "

You can *agree in principle* when you agree with the logic of your critic although not necessarily with his or her premise. If can agree that "If X, then Y," without agreeing that "X" is true.

> A: "If you don't study more, you're going to fail."
> B: "You're right, if I don't study, I will fail."

You are not agreeing that you should necessarily study more. You are agreeing with the connection between studying and failing or succeeding.

You could then add my favorite, "You could be right" and the speaker will feel heard AND validated. You, on the other hand, have made no concessions, nor taken any prisoners!

Ask for what you need and want

Do not hedge or hint . . . ASK! You have the right and the responsibility to speak up for yourself in every way. When you are feeling most pressured, you may feel less forceful. This is the prime time to speak your truth and be totally kind in the process. Those are the skills that this book is intended to convey.

You are not there to usurp the rights of another. You are there to stand up for what you need and want while listening and responding to the needs and wants of others.

> **Hold up your end of the bargain! You'll feel better.**
> **You'll be more likely to get what you want.**
> **You'll have no regrets. What a deal!**

**Negotiation in the classic diplomatic
sense assumes parties more anxious
to agree than to disagree.**

Dean Acheson

FAILURE TO NEGOTIATE IS A SURE NO-WIN

If you do nothing, the ball is always in the other person's court! Are you giving up your ability to make a difference for yourself in the relationships in your life?

In my negotiation seminar, I talk about the five choices we have in any conflict situation: yield, collaborate, compromise, avoid, compete. Each is a good strategy . . . sometimes!

Of course, it is wise to pick your battles. Some things simply do not matter much to you. Yielding is fine. When your negotiating partner really cares about something and it's relatively immaterial to you, yield. That's wise. (By the way, if you find yourself wanting to win even in these situations, you may need to consider counseling. That's a sign that you missed something along the way and maturity is not on your side.)

Avoidance is another matter. There is wisdom in avoidance when the timing of a conflict is very wrong, or the person is your superior and your job is on the line. If your negotiating partner is very upset, angry, or out of control, this is not the time! It does not mean that the conversation will be postponed indefinitely. When emotions are high, negotiating will not likely be anything resembling rational. That is a good time to practice avoidance.

Negotiating with your boss or supervisor requires good communication and negotiation skills . . . and maximum preparation. Unless you want to be miserable forever, I don't recommend continuing to avoid talking with him or her. But it does require some careful thought and consideration.

Remember that staggering statistic,

> " . . . except for people moving on to better positions, salaries, or new fields, 80% of people interviewed were leaving their jobs because of expressed, or unexpressed, interpersonal conflict!"

That's huge. It speaks of an entire working population with poor conflict management skills.

Stand out. Be the person with the well-honed skills, and life will be a much more rewarding and satisfying experience.

Compromise is over-rated. It means that both people had to give up something that they really wanted. Sure, there are incidents where this is appropriate. You may do it because the other person is so important to you that you want them to have what they most want. You take the loss magnanimously. Usually, though, it is because you do not know how to negotiate. And, usually, you are keeping score.

Be careful. *Do not use compromise as a substitute for negotiation.* Repeated use may be addicting and will keep you angry.

Competition can be healthy. It requires staying in shape to compete– physical, emotional, intellectual, social shape. And, comes with a caveat: **You compete FOR things and positions, not WITH people.** Don't you hate it when political candidates start taking swipes at folks, badmouthing them, pointing out their faults? That is because they are competing *with* people rather than *for* issues. That's why competition has a bad rep!

Competition has a huge drawback. It is the most likely approach to destroy a relationship! It is based on satisfying our own concerns while ignoring the other's goals, needs or issues. It jeopardizes any on-going relationship possibilities. It will end in a definite win-lose. Useful in buying a new car, destructive with your cubicle mate or life partner!

That leaves us with collaborate, the integrative approach. It takes into consideration the needs, concerns, desires, and wants of both parties and offers the most lasting, positive results.

In truth, it isn't what the other person wants but *why they want it* that is important. When we take the time to hear the compelling reasons behind someone's request, it changes things. This is the beginning of collaboration. It requires excellent listening skills. You're not just listening to the words, but to the feelings and thinking behind the words.

This is not a time to operate from assumptions. In all negotiations, test for accuracy. State what you have heard and ask if you have the information straight. This demonstrates your willingness to communicate which is the basis for negotiation.

People with poorly thought-out positions compete or avoid. Wise folks collaborate. It preserves, and even strengthens, on-going relationships.

If you do not negotiate, you have made a decision in favor of the status quo. That could be wise. It could be foolish. It could be that the thought of negotiation scares you rigid.

One thing is sure:
Failure to negotiate is a sure no-win . . . and not in your favor!

**In business, you don't get what you
deserve, you get what you negotiate.**

Chester L. Karrass

GET INTO THE HABIT OF ASKING FOR WHAT YOU WANT

John wanted a particular week off in the summer to attend a family reunion. It was particularly important to him for two reasons: for the first time, every single member of the family would be there, and it would be on Maui. He checked the office schedule and found that another member of his team had already booked the same time away. Disappointedly he told his family he could not attend. The answer he accepted was no.

The truth was that the co-worker who booked that time off had chosen her week off at random. A simple request from John would have been all that was required for her to change her dates. What was going on here?

History may have told you that asking may be difficult, timing may be tricky, and receiving may be unlikely, but if you do not ask, the answer will always be no!

EXPECTATIONS

Our expectations in any relationship are based on history, on how things have worked in the past. Interestingly, we will even take *someone else's history* as evidence. Does this make sense? Sometimes, yes, and sometimes, no.

There are very few true *laws*. People do not do the same things in the same ways with the same people, in every case. Yet often we behave as though this is true. If it happened once, it will always happen! If it happened to someone, it will happen to me.

Sure, it makes sense to stay away from sharks. They usually attack and you look like food. As there is likely no good reason to approach a shark, there is no problem. What, though, if that shark had your daughter's arm in its mouth? You would likely take some action to get what you want.

The same is true at the office. When something is important to you and contributes to your well-being, it requires action.

RELATIONSHIPS

It's true that we are most comfortable asking the people we know least and those we know best when there is something we want. It's simply easiest!

Folks unknown to you come with no expectation of outcome. Rejection from them is easier to handle. Folks you know well will either give you what you want or, at least, soften their refusal by taking care of the relationship. It's those in-between folks that are daunting.

When you ask someone for help, you are telling that person you believe they have the skills or experience to give you that help. Don't you feel good when someone asks for your help? (Of course, we're not talking about those few folks who are always asking for it—those who are too lazy, too needy, or too demanding.)

You can enhance a relationship by asking for help. You open the relationship to become more reciprocal. That's a choice only you can determine is appropriate. If you do not want to be asked for something, best not be asking others yourself!

But, again, if you do not ask, the answer is always "No!"

APPROACH

Some ways of approaching an issue are more productive than others. It's unlikely you'll get what you want by beginning with "I'm sure you'll say no, but . . . " You may have tried that one when you were a teenager. It didn't work well, did it?

- Be prepared
- Be ready to ask clearly for what you want
- Know why you want it
- Be prepared with benefits to the listener for giving you what you are requesting

If possible, give them a plan that will work for them . . . and for you. When you do the work, you're more likely to get what you want.

Pick your moment carefully.
Check.

> "I would like to discuss something with you. Is this a good time?"

or

> "When would you have a few minutes free to discuss something?"

If you are asking a supervisor or manager, they will likely want to know what the topic is. This is fair, however, how you answer is important. It can make all the difference between getting the meeting or not.

Phrase your issue broadly and positively.

> "I'd like to discuss the vacation schedule."

rather than,

> "I need to talk to you about getting the dates I want for vacation."

Give the overall topic, not your specific request. If pressed for specifics, again be positive, clear, and brief.

JUST DO IT

Once in the meeting:

- ✦ First, thank him or her for their time.
- ✦ Give the benefits to the listener for giving you what you want, then ask.
- ✦ Ask clearly for exactly what you want.
- ✦ Do not apologize for your request. You have the right to ask as they have the right to refuse.
- ✦ Whatever the outcome, the relationship will shift slightly no matter who you ask for what!
- ✦ Again, be prepared.

You have probably heard the English proverb:

"Most things are lost for want of asking."

There is no need to lose anything for that reason. Simply ask. You may be surprised how easy this becomes with practice.

**Remember, though, if you do not ask,
the answer is always no. So, ask!**

KNOW WHEN TO HOLD
AND WHEN TO FOLD

Preparation is key to any negotiation. If you have not done your homework, *your own work*, prior to talking with your negotiating partner, you risk a great deal. You have to be as ready as possible on all levels.

> **The fellow who says he'll meet you halfway usually thinks he's standing on the dividing line.**
>
> Orlando A. Battista

Know what you want and why you want it. It is your compelling reasons for wanting it that will keep you focused and clear in the negotiation process. Just as in goal-setting, it will be your reasons for wanting to reach the goal that will carry you towards it. The goal itself is simply a benchmark for the underlying reasons. In negotiation, the same is true. Stay focused on *why* and the *what* will be easier to maintain.

Before you enter any negotiation, you need to know three important things:

- ✦ Your IDEAL outcome
- ✦ Your ACCEPTABLE outcome
- ✦ Your WALKAWAY

First, **know what you want and be willing to ask for it.** Think big and make your request. This is what you think you deserve at the maximum level.

John F. Kennedy said,

> "Let us never negotiate out of fear. But, let us never fear to negotiate."

An executive coaching client of mine was sought out by a competitor of her employer. Would she consider coming to work for them? The job description was appealing. The location was of interest. The responsibilities were huge.

As we worked through the pros and cons, I encouraged her to decide on her ideal salary. Several times she was tempted to set her ideal at what she thought she could get. WRONG!

> "Ask for what you truly believe you are worth and for what you most want."

I encouraged her. It was difficult for her, however, she did see the wisdom in it. So, she asked for $165,000. Her potential boss said,

> "Good. That's not too far from what I was thinking. I can give you $150,000 with a $25,000 bonus in the first year."

Now, that was quite an excellent result and it all came from having the gumption to ask for her IDEAL outcome.

Preparation takes the fear out of negotiation. That client was prepared. She worked out her insecurities and worked through her limited expectations. She knew that her ACCEPTABLE outcome was $140,000. She is delighted with her negotiated outcome.

The toughest part in the negotiation process, for most folks, is the WALKAWAY. They want to make nice, make it work, have people like them . . . choose one. The truth is they simply do not have the strength of their conviction that they are worth having their desired outcomes. So, they settle for less.

I believe that no one should ever negotiate if they are not willing to walk away without a deal. If you will not walk away empty handed by your choice, you will walk away with less than you wanted and more resentment than you can handle! Has it happened to you? Did it damage a relationship? In all likelihood, it did.

Once again, you are 100% in charge of teaching people how to treat you. Remember that, too, when you are negotiating.

Negotiation is the highest form of communication used by the lowest number of people.

John F. Kennedy

STEPS TO EFFECTIVE NEGOTIATION

Negotiation is a fact of life. Little children learn about it early. You did, too. Were you effective? Are you now? Do you want to improve your abilities? Feel better about both the outcome and yourself when negotiating? You can.

Effective negotiation is not a contest of wills to determine who has the most power. It is not a game in which each party seeks to best the other. But, there are rules! Rules that make the dialogue respectful and the outcomes fair.

> During a negotiation, it would be wise not to take anything personally. If you leave personalities out of it, you will be able to see opportunities more objectively.
>
> Brian Koslow

In *Getting to Yes, Negotiating Agreement Without Giving In*[1], Roger Fisher and William Ury of the **Harvard Negotiation Project** tell us that there are four main keys to successful negotiation.

1. PEOPLE

Separate the people from the issues. There is no need to personalize the issues with remarks about the person on the other side of the table. Stick to the issues.

Recognize that there is emotion and investment on both sides and be prepared to listen well. You know what Steven Covey says,

'Seek first to understand, then to be understood'.

Be soft on people and hard on issues. This way you can keep the relationship AND a mutually satisfying outcome.

2. INTERESTS

Focus on the interests of the other, rather than the position. Behind each position lies compatible as well as conflicting interests. For example, when negotiating a raise, a wise person acknowledges that the interests of the company are to be progressive while making a profit.

The wise boss acknowledges the interests of the employee to accelerate on his/her career path while making a contribution to the company and supporting his/her lifestyle or family.

**Negotiations do not take place in a vacuum.
Each person has a real life going on, with real needs and interests.**

3. OPTIONS

Work with the other party to generate a variety of options from which to create a solution. Brainstorm possibilities without judgment or comment. You'll be surprised how many good ideas can surface when this is allowed to occur.

Make no decisions until you've exhausted your list of possibilities. Then, look for areas of agreement. Where are your interests shared? Where are the interests a good fit? Explore options that are of low cost to you and high value to the other party and vice versa.

4. CRITERIA

It is imperative to negotiate within mutually agreed-upon standards of fairness. Otherwise, egotiating can turn to street-fighting! These criteria may range from current market value to procedures for resolving conflict. They will allow you to create an equitable solution while keeping your relationship intact. Want proof? Try it at home!

Negotiating fairly builds trust. Demonstrations of power erode it.

Before beginning to negotiate, decide on the ground rules and stick to them. You are setting the standard for future conversations as well. Remember, you teach people how to treat you in two ways: you set and enforce your boundaries, and you demonstrate your values in the ways you treat others. I cannot say this often enough!

Bargaining ridiculously and maintaining strong positions are best left for those fun holiday moments when you do not really care whether or not the street vendor sells you that black velvet painting. In the business world, those tactics may bring you short-term results, however, the long-term damage to the relationships involved may be too costly.

Remember, wherever there is a winner, there must be a loser. Hard-nosed bargaining usually leaves both sides exhausted, resentful, and dissatisfied. You may know this from bitter experience. You'll especially relate to this if you were on the losing end!

Wise negotiators make wise concessions so that their negotiating partners never feel like losers. Take a page from their book!

NEGOTIATE WELL:

- ♦ Be clear about the outcome you prefer
- ♦ Be able to express this preference well with supporting statements that will make sense to your partner

- ⊕ Be prepared to listen more than, or at least as much as, you speak
- ⊕ Listen for common interests and possible options
- ⊕ Know what you are willing to give as well as what you would like to receive

When you are focused this way, you will get more of what you want, more often, while winning friends and influencing people. What a compelling reason for integrating the rules into your next negotiation!

1. Roger Fisher and William Ury. *Getting to Yes: Negotiating Agreement Without Giving In.* (New York: Penguin Books, 1991 [Houghton-Mifflin 1981])

RULES, REMNANTS & RUMINATIONS:

UNCOMMON COMMON SENSE FOR WORKING WELL TOGETHER

Imagine life as a game in which you are juggling some five balls in the air. You name them . . . work, family, health, friends, and spirit, and you're keeping all of these in the air. You will soon understand that work is a rubber ball. If you drop it, it will bounce back.
But the other four balls . . . family, health, friends and spirit . . . are made of glass.
If you drop one of these, they will be irrevocably scuffed, marked, nicked, damaged, or even shattered. They will never be the same.

Anonymous

HOW TO OVERTHROW OVERWHELM

Did this ever happen to you? You were learning to swim and found yourself underwater, gasping for breath and struggling for the surface. Do you remember that feeling?

Isn't that just like the feeling of overwhelm in daily life? We are gasping for breath and struggling to maintain our "surface", the façade that we have it all together.

Oh, now there's a clue. The clue is in the difference. When we were learning to swim, we struggled to get up to the surface to be safe. In overwhelm, we struggle to maintain the "surface" to feel safe. Very different in motivation.

What is a surface? It is both the exterior or upper boundary of an object or body AND the external or superficial aspect of something. Bingo! Now it makes sense. The surface of the water is something we want to break through. The surface we create in life may equate to some ruler we've adopted to measure our worth. And, superficial may be just the right word to describe it.

Could it be possible that the very busy lives most folks lead are kept spinning faster and faster to meet someone else's arbitrary measure of what is *good enough*? Think of the old saying, "keeping up with the Joneses." That expression was invented by a comic-strip artist, Arthur R. "Pop" Momand in the *New York Globe* in 1913. It was based on the artist's own attempts to keep up with his neighbors.

In this global economy, that bar has been raised. Our neighbors may be every successful, wealthy, accomplished achiever ever interviewed for TV or *People Magazine*. We may have unconsciously accepted the challenge to meet or beat the Joneses without knowing them or understanding if what they have achieved has made them happy. We may make assumptions that if we had what the Joneses had, did what the Joneses did, went to the same schools or belonged to the same clubs as the Joneses, or were the same kinds of people as the Joneses, we would be happier. Or, maybe, better. Or, maybe at least, good enough.

It is important and fundamentally worthwhile to cut yourself some quiet time and think about the answers to the following questions.

WHAT IS IMPORTANT, SIGNIFICANT AND VALUABLE TO YOU?

Careful now. Guard against rhyming off the things you think are *supposed* to be all those things to you. Often those quick lists are the Joneses speaking! Reflect on the question further.

- ⬥ How would you like to be described by the people who are most important to you?
- ⬥ What brings you joy?
- ⬥ What gives you satisfaction?
- ⬥ How are your relationships and how would you like them to be?

There are no right answers, only *your* answers. Those are the only ones that are right for you.

I remember in one of my seminars I noticed a man with tears streaming quietly down his face. When everyone else was talking together, I asked him what the source of his tears was. He said that it had hit him all of a sudden that he had been living his life for the approval of others, that he had lost sight of what he most wanted. He was grieving the loss of that part of himself and the time lost in that pursuit.

Let's not be like that man. Let's take the time today to honestly look at what we're doing and assess if it is our own conscious choice, or one that we have accepted from the Joneses.

HOW DOES YOUR LIFE REFLECT YOUR ANSWERS?

There is one quick way to assess how closely your life reflects what is closest to your heart. Check your checkbook and your calendar. I've mentioned this in other articles you'll find on my website. (www.OptimizeInstitute.com) This is key!

It's easy to say that you value your family above anything else. When you look at your calendar, you may be surprised how little time is carved out each week to demonstrate this.

It's also easy to say that self-development is important to you. Can you clearly see where you have invested time and money in books, CDs, classes, or seminars in the last six months? Of course, buying and attending things only *looks* like progress. (And, thanks for buying this book!) Apparently you know you actually have to read the books, listen to the CDs, and implement the seminar strategies, too. Sure, there are other ways to measure these things, however, these two will get you thinking. Begin there.

HOW CAN YOU OVERTHROW OVERWHELM?

Get your ducks in a row! Live from your own expectations, not those of others. Choose things to be, do, and have in your life consciously, not because some TV ad or famous person said it was a good thing. Choose it because it is right for you. Before you begin to feel pressured, take time for yourself. Set goals that demonstrate balance.

Not long ago I was coaching a young woman on the phone. I had never met her in person and that was our first session. On the pre-session questionnaire, I noticed that she rated her focusing, planning, and organizing skills very high. Then, I looked at her family life, fun life, and social life scores. All very low. What's up with that?

When we began to talk, she described how she is completely focused on her career and feels guilty if she even stops to exercise. Driven to succeed in business, all her time, energy, and focus is there. When I asked her about the inequity of the two sets of scores, she was quick to tell me that she simply could not do it any other way because she simply HAD to establish her career and make a lot of money. Then, she said, she would be able to relax and achieve some balance in her life.

She was noticeably quiet when I asked her this question:

> "How will your career be affected when you go through your divorce and/or become very ill?"

Being a bright, young woman, she got the picture immediately. Great start! It's just a beginning, though.

Awareness is the first step. Change requires vigilant attention.

What is overwhelm about? The word actually means *"to cover over completely or submerge."* There we are, gasping for air, drowning in a sea of our own making. Oh, it would be so easy to find relationships, events, and demands to blame. It wouldn't be true, though.

Each one of us has one hundred and sixty-eight hours in our week. Each one of us decides how to spend those hours—either consciously or unconsciously.

Now, now, don't go there! There is no special-interest, special-circumstance pleading allowed in this case. At some level, in some way, you have DECIDED to accept, create, or tolerate these thing in your life. Yes, you. Overthrow overwhelm by taking back your life. Stop. Step off the merry-go-round.

✦ Look to see if your current "brass rings" are worth reaching for.

✦ Do YOU value them?

- ⊕ Will they truly make your life satisfying and worthwhile?
- ⊕ What are they costing you?
- ⊕ Is it worth it?

Now, make a plan. At this time of your life, what is most important? Adjust your checkbook and calendar to reflect this within one month. Keep that commitment to yourself. You can have it all. You just can't have it all at once and keep your sanity.

One day my daughter, one of my best creative acts, asked me to write her a "something to remember," and I wrote this:

"What is important is simple:
Know what you value and invest your time accordingly.
This is integrity and it will bring you peace."

That's the surest way I know to overthrow overwhelm.
So, Optimize Life Now!

Real heroes are men [people] who fall and fail and are flawed, but win out in the end because they've stayed true to their ideals and beliefs and commitments.

Kevin Costner

PREVENTING BURNOUT

We get burned when we stay too close to a heat source for too long. Wise folks move away before they get burned, but some are so focused on other things that they fail to feel the heat! When the heat finally gets their attention, they can barely crawl away to safety. They suffer from burnout. Too much, too little, too late, too long. Those are what define burnout.

TOO MUCH

You do and you do and you do. You are the one who can be counted on to stay late, come in early, skip lunch, and pick up the pieces when others let them fall. In fact, *people begin to count on you to do just that*! This is a recipe for burnout.

You've read in other chapters that you are one hundred percent responsible for teaching people how to treat you. There it is again. Have you taught other people to treat you as a safety plug, or a backup plan? Who is responsible for that? You! Oh, and you thought that *indispensable* was a sure-fire strategy for promotion? Wrong. It is a strategy for burnout.

You thought that going the extra mile was just good exercise. It's exhausting done daily. Save it for times when you will be appreciated, not taken for granted.

TOO LITTLE

I was working with a coaching client and she said,

> "I've given my life to this company and my reward is a pink slip."

Oops! Mistake. She only has one life and she needs to keep it for herself. Work is only a part of life and it must be kept within the confines of values and goals. I don't know one person who has consciously set the goal to be the first in the company to experience burnout. Yet, paying too little attention to maintaining healthy balance is the equivalent. Any good manager wants you to be living a balanced life. Why? So that when a little extra is required, it's available. If you're running as fast as you can every day, you have nothing left for an occasional sprint to a deadline.

TOO LATE

Sometimes you don't realize all that you are giving until it's too late! The greatest weapon you have against burnout is a simple one. Gently pucker your lips, open your mouth, and speak that self-saving word.

Whether it's work-related, family-related, or expectation-driven, you have to learn to say "NO!" before it is too late. You cannot be all things to all people all the time.

Practice on small things. If a person asks you to go somewhere that you do not want to go, thank them for wanting to do something that includes you and say, "NO!" If you haven't tried this, it takes a little practice . . . and no one has ever died from doing it. Just practice. It gets easier. Remember, too, that you never need to give a reason or an excuse. A simple "NO, THANKS." is all that is required . . . with a smile. And yes, "No." is a complete sentence.

TOO LONG

The body and mind are resilient and forgiving . . . to a point! You can push on through a whole night's work and recover quite quickly in a day or two of rest. No problem. Burnout occurs when pushing becomes a lifestyle. Do more. Be more. Have more. Rescue more. Work more. Accommodate more. Push, push, push. The body simply cannot handle the demand and the fuses blow. A medical dictionary says that burnout is

> " . . . an excessive stress reaction to one's occupational or professional environment. It is manifested by feelings of emotional and physical exhaustion coupled with a sense of frustration and failure."[1]

Those feelings come from the blown fuses. Physically, you can go into meltdown. Your adrenals are distressed. Your skin is rebelling. Your stomach produces excess acid. Your sleep is disturbed. Everything is stressed beyond reason and all you want to do is crawl in a hole and pull the hole in after you for a long, long rest.

GOOD NEWS! You can avoid all this. It's a choice.
So, if you recognize a "too much, too little, too late, too long" kind
of build-up in yourself, STOP! Choose health instead.

1. Health Communication Network. http://www.hcn.com.au

Be so strong that nothing can disturb your
peace of mind.
Talk health, happiness, and prosperity to
every person you meet.
Make all your friends feel there is something
in them.
Look at the sunny side of everything.
Think only of the best, work only for the best,
and expect only the best.
Be as enthusiastic about the success of
others as you are about your won.
Forget the mistakes of the past and press on
to the greater achievements of the future.
Give everyone a smile.
Spend so much time improving yourself that
you have no time left to criticize others.
Be too big for worry and too noble for anger.

Christian D. Larsen (Creed for Optimists)

ANY UNFINISHED BUSINESS?

Energy leaks fall into the category of "Unfinished Business." *Procrastination is a major energy leak.* So is denial. The reason many people don't deal, or won't deal, with this unfinished business is fear. Fear leads to doubt which leads eventually to lack of confidence. This can become an even bigger problem as you can begin to feel out of control. This creates anxiety and soon the energy leak becomes a flood.

You can have a tremendous amount of unfinished business over the years. Maybe it's time to put a stop to those leaks. Sure, it will take energy, but, energy expended to stop the leaks will prevent drowning in that flood.

It will not be useful to build a dam. The maintenance of a dam is just another energy leak. You may have already tried to build a dam. You do that by simply denying that the problem, issue, or request exists. Living in a fantasy world usually ends in disaster . . . or medication. Neither of those are acceptable alternatives.

It will not be useful to tread water, either. You expend so much energy just trying to keep pace that, not only do you not get anywhere, you are fatigued. You're frustrated, and, you're still stuck.

The only useful approach is to have a good look at the leaks and fix them one at a time. Now this is easy if the leak is simply an unpaid parking ticket. You write the check, put it in an envelope, affix the stamp and mail it. Done! What if it is a relationship that is draining you?

First, spend some time determining what changes you want. Then, ask that other person if they are able or willing to meet your need. Be ready to hear both yes and no. That's so important. You know that you cannot force someone to change, so *you* may have to be ready to change—even ready to change relationships!

Do you have issues at work? Are you in the best job for you? This can be draining your energy. Many times, difficult relationships at work are not well-managed. These are leaks, too.

You may have an old issue that needs resolving. Do you need to apologize to someone, or ask for forgiveness? This is the time. It is draining your energy every time you think about it! You know what Nike says, "Just Do It!™"

Sure, you may be fearful. That's natural. It's likely, though, that your imagination has created a much bigger obstacle than the actual event will be! Your fear is devouring too much energy. Do it! Face the music! Go through it! Be done with it.

Whatever you have been putting off or "forgetting," refuse to let it drain another erg from you.
Put an end to unfinished business NOW. Wrestle that rhino!

MOUNTAIN CLIMBING OVER MOLEHILLS

Someone has said that the greatest cause of ulcers is mountain-climbing over molehills! Is that the way you get your exercise?

Many folks allow themselves to be thrown off course by minor or imaginary threats. Often they interpret these as life-or-death, or do-or-die situations. They put so much energy into their worries that there is no energy available for progress. Some people believe that worrying demonstrates caring. This is misguided, too.

> **Worry compounds the futility of being trapped on a dead-end street. Thinking opens new avenues.**
>
> Cullen Hightower

The use you make of your energy is your choice. Simply use it consciously and constructively. Worry is neither.

Bertrand Russell, philosopher and mathematician, tells of a technique he used on himself to calm down his worries and excessive negative excitement:

> "When some misfortune threatens, consider seriously and deliberately what is the very worst that could possibly happen. Having looked this possible misfortune in the face, give yourself sound reasons for thinking that after all it would be no such very terrible disaster. Such reasons always exist, since at the worst, nothing that happens to oneself has any cosmic importance. When you have looked for some time steadily at the worst possibility and have said to yourself with real conviction, 'Well, after all, that would not matter so very much,' you will find that your worry diminishes to a quite extraordinary extent. It may be necessary to repeat the process a few times, but in the end, if you have shirked nothing in facing the worse possible issue, you will find that your worry disappears altogether and is replaced by a kind of exhilaration."[1]

Now that seems worth having. *Exhilaration brings energy to push through difficulties and to level mountains as well as mole-hills.*

This strategy for approaching your concerns can help you to maintain an assertive, goal-directed, self-determining attitude even in the presence of very real and serious threats and dangers.

Abandon denial. Take positive action.

1. Bertrand Russell. *The Conquest of Happiness.* (New York: H. Liveright, 1930).

MATURITY OR JUST LONGEVITY?

Are there folks in your organization who believe in the *longevity model*? Likely there are. These are the people who learned their jobs really well in the first year of employment and continue to repeat that same year over and over and over. **Perfectly pleasant people performing patiently!**

> **Maturity includes the recognition that no one is going to see anything in us that we don't see in ourselves. Stop waiting for a producer. Produce yourself.**
>
> Marianne Williamson

One time, I was training a team in the public sector on the topic "Be Promotable." In working with the human resources folks, I asked,

"What would you really like your employees to understand from this seminar?"

One response was that individuals had to realize that simply repeating tasks and occupying a seat on a regular basis would only lead them to the possibility of continuing to occupy that particular seat! **People are not promoted for demonstrating the longevity model.**

This is an important shift to notice in the work world of today.

Whether you are a Pre-boomer, a Baby boomer, or a buster, a Generation X or Y, you can count on one thing: Your work ethic will not be the same as folks of other ages within your organization.

Your expectations will be different and your model will have been shaped by those expectations.

There was a day, not too long ago, when workplace loyalty was a deciding factor. When someone demonstrated loyalty by working well for the same company for a long time, they were rewarded by promotion. In fact, they expected it. That was the way things were done. It was not necessarily loyalty to a concept or a person, it was a generalized loyalty demonstrated by showing up, accomplishing the work, and occupying that seat over a long period of time. Of course, I'm simplifying this to make my point.

These days, loyalty is more likely to be demonstrated to an idea, a concept, a product, or a person than to a commitment for the long haul. Whereas once folks had one career, the average these days is three to five careers. Current research tells us that, in order to move up in your career, you will likely change positions or companies every two to five years. Not only that, the research suggests you MUST do that to progress. That is a major shift, isn't it? And, it has taken place within thirty years. *There has been huge change in a short time in the way work is perceived.*

So the longevity model no longer applies to our marketplace. We need the **maturity model** which exists when employees are learning, growing, AND applying new information while taking responsibility for their roles, tasks, and progress. These folks understand the meaning of accountability. That's big!

I was working with a department of a large public sector organization. The fundamental task I had was to shift and secure their existing model to one of maturity. The dictionary defines "mature" as *of or relating to a condition of full development.*

That's what we're after in the workplace: full development.

- ✛ What would it be like if "full development" was the desire and goal of each and every worker?
- ✛ What would it be like if this was both the desire and commitment of every employer?
- ✛ What if every employee AND every member of management were truly accountable?

Folks Would Work For The Hours For Which They Are Paid.

When you take a position, you know the hours, the benefits, the job description, and the compensation. That means that you then undertake to do those things for that long to reap those benefits and take home that compensation. Simple equation. Many folks understand it completely. There are some, though, that seem to take up the challenge of seeing how little they can do without being noticed. They even seem to think that the organization provides them with a telephone and e-mail so that they can stay in touch with their friends and fill their social calendars.

One employee in a firm I worked with actually stated that she came to work as a respite from her home life and her home-based business! Very often she could be found chatting in hallways and cubicles about her children, husband, and health rather than focusing on her work and supervising her staff.

Folks Would Fulfill, And Even Exceed, Their Job Descriptions.

In the ideal world, your acceptance of your paycheck is your statement of fulfilling your job description. Too obvious? Perhaps.

Accountability requires that you:

- ✛ Take the initiative to learn your tasks
- ✛ Ask questions
- ✛ Read books
- ✛ Keep up with your industry by reading newsletters and trade journals

✦ Request training and use it well

Knowing your job reduces your stress. Exceeding your job's expectations leads to promotion.

Folks Would Be Respectful Of Time, Energy, Resources, And Finances.

✦ Be on time to meetings. It demonstrates respect.

✦ Honor timelines and deadlines. It creates high-performance.

✦ Conserve resources and money wisely to improve the bottom line.

Simple. But, why do it? In large companies I have heard employees say that it doesn't matter much if they make an error because the company will never notice, or because the company has so much money it wouldn't matter. Wrong. It's not about that. *It is about you being accountable for the choices you make which demonstrate your commitment to doing the best job possible.*

**These ARE the things that are noticed.
Which model are you? Longevity or maturity?**

**It's your choice . . .
and, of course, so are the consequences!**

YOUR JOB:
WHEN YOU DON'T LOVE IT,
BUT CANNOT LEAVE IT

I was talking with a coaching client who is a VP of Sales and Marketing. Great job. The position utilizes her best skills and she has made her company fifteen times her salary this year so far. Great result. So, what is the problem?

She does not love the job, the location, or the boss. Three strikes against it and she needs to stay in the game. Sure, she has discreetly spoken to recruiters in several states. She regularly gets e-mail from all the major websites with job offerings. She has contacted all those fine people in her network in several cities. And, she's waiting . . . and waiting.

> I've met a few people who had to change their jobs in order to change their lives, but I've met many more people who merely had to change their motive to service in order to change their lives.
>
> Peace Pilgrim

We know the job market can seem little tight—more than a little in some markets. What to do? Old wisdom suggests that if you can't love the one you want, love the one you're with. There might be something to that in the world of work.

⊕ What percentage of your time are you finding fault compared with time spent looking for ways to make a creative contribution?

⊕ What percentage of your energy is absorbed in how much you dislike your situation compared with filling your time by doing the best job possible?

Perspective is everything. And this simple shift is a survival tactic that will support you in every area of your life. After all, how miserable you become is your choice.

You know that what you pay attention to expands. You know that's true because if you buy a new Miata, all of a sudden you see them everywhere. Why? Because you became aware of them in a new way and now you see them more readily. The same is true with the faults of folks you work with or live with. The more attention you place on them, the bigger they seem. Did you ever, all of sudden, become aware of the sound some makes when they are eating? Once you do, it's often impossible to hear anything else!

First, Focus

Focus on what you can change about yourself. Can you place your energy and attention on projects that allow you to demonstrate your skills and abilities? Then do it. Can you remember who and how you want to be in the face of the smallness of others? Practice that.

Be scrupulous in the way you observe yourself and your current work ethic. One survey reported 85% of respondents said they were not giving their best at work. Wow! No wonder it's tough getting service in most places! Be one of the 15% focused on giving your employer value for the money they exchange for the hours you work. You're working on your work ethic, improving your marketability. When you do leave, your employer will have much better things to say about you when you've given great value. After all, it's just YOUR reputation.

Then, Communicate

Is there someone you can talk to in the workplace who has the power to improve things? Beware of office chatter and gossip. Only speak about issues to people who can do something about them. The rest is idle, energy-draining, time-wasting talk. Keep away from it!

If possible, take your problem directly to the person *with whom you have the problem* first. If a co-worker is not pulling his weight, speak to him first. Tell him how making a change would benefit him and what would work for you. Do this with an attitude of team play rather than competitive righteousness. You know what I mean: no control tactics or one-upmanship, just low-key conversation with a strong intent to improve things between you.

If necessary, then (and only then), take it up a notch. Speak to your superior and ask for guidance. Notice, it's not a let-me-tell-you-this-about-her and how-she-needs-to-get-her-act-together' kind of talk. Ask for help. That is a good way of letting your supervisor or manager know there is an issue without drama and exaggeration. If the guidance you receive is "Put up with it," then return to item one and focus on yourself.

Clarify

Know what you want and learn to ask for it in ways that make people want to provide it for you. Be clear and specific. Once you have communicated your request—note: request, not demand—ask the person if they are willing and able to meet it. That's a fair question. Be ready to hear either Yes or No. At least you will have further information to make your decisions easier.

Now, if, after all this, nothing changes you're back to two choices once again. *Stick it out or stick it.* At least you'll know that you've given your best effort and folks know where you stand. You'll have had great practice with positive strategies and you will have been pro-active.

You know what Henry Ford said, "Think you can or think you can't, either way you'll be right." The same is true about your job.

The more energy you give to what you don't like about something, the more miserable it becomes. It's your choice!

**The greatest revolution of our
generation is the discovery that
human beings, by changing the inner
attitudes of their minds, can change
the outer aspects of their lives.**

William James

TAKE YOUR FINGERS OFF IT, PUH-LEASE!

H as anyone ever asked you to take on a task or project and then hovered over you while you did it? That can be so annoying! It is imperative that folks learn to delegate in the true sense of word. It means *to entrust to another*. Being hovered over does not seem to embody the essence of trust by any means.

You are the manager and you know you need to delegate some parts of your project. Your reputation or credibility is on the line. Your promotion may depend on it, so, naturally, you are reluctant to keep your fingers out of the project. No matter how difficult it seems, you must think about the long-term relationships you are creating. Those people who are working for you to make that big impression are the same people you are likely going to need again. If you have explained the project accurately, emphasized the need for the deadline to be met, and, you have their agreement and understanding, your job is to get on with the parts of the project that only you can do. Trust your staff.

When you delegate a task, be sure to take enough time in the initial conversation to assure yourself that the person can, in fact, do the task. Then, agree on the details and deadlines. Have regular meetings for progress reports, questions and support. That will eliminate concern for everyone. But, don't be sitting over their shoulders every minute. Your anxiety over the success of the project will not be well-served by making everyone else anxious.

Are you being hovered over? Two questions to ask yourself: do you believe you can do the task without supervision, and, do you understand the fear your project manager has?

If you are comfortable with the task, tell your manager.

> "I know this project is very important to you. I want you to know that I can do this for you and I can do it on time. I hope that will free you up to focus on other aspects of the project."

You'll often find that just bringing up the underlying fear and giving it a name can change the dynamics. By offering assurance in this form, you have supported your manager without complaining about the hovering. Be pro-active and save both of you some irritation and anxiety.

Learning to delegate is one of the most difficult things new managers can face. It feels like giving away control and that can be daunting. Front load the issue. Take the time to talk out the project and make agreements about format, style, timelines, and desired outcomes. Then, take your fingers off it, puh-lease!

Once project parameters are set and agreed to, giving the respect and allowing the "space" for a job to be done is the surest way to get the best job done.

WHEN IN DOUBT, MOVE ON OUT!

Are you working for a manager or supervisor who is moving forward in the company? Great. Does he or she like you? Terrific. Does your boss introduce you to her peers? Even better. Are you invited to join special meetings and task forces? Marvelous. Will your boss trust you to do parts of his job for him? Perfect! Why are these things important? These are clear signs that you are in the right place to be promoted.

If you want a career, you must have designed a career path, otherwise you have a job. If that is satisfying to you and suits your values and preferred lifestyle, you are doing everything right. If you want to move forward and up, you must clarify your career goals and design your blueprint for success.

- ⊕ Do you clearly know what you want to achieve?
- ⊕ Have you examined your lifestyle and your working style to see that this is a good fit for you?

Many folks don't. They see the power, glamour, or control inherent in a certain position and want those things without understanding themselves well enough to know if that will work for them.

I was consulting with a department within a large firm. There were several issues causing conflict and low productivity. My task was to meet with individuals, find the issues from their points-of-view, and design and implement training to overcome the inertia. The training began with an inventory** each person took to assess their personal core values at work. What a wonderful day we had as the light bulbs went on around the room! I heard things like,

> "Oh, that's why I find getting that done so difficult."
> "No wonder we are at each others' throats."
> "Wow, our boss is so different from us in style that he can't possibly understand us easily."

Knowing what is significant, important and valuable to you before designing your career path is essential.

An enlightened company that wants to maximize the productivity and effectiveness of its employees would be interested in creating ideal job profiles—finding the person who best fits the position in working and learning style. That's why I recommend companies to use the inventory** I use to improve current work groups as well as to define up-coming positions. It saves time and energy, tears and money! Who wouldn't want to do that?

Are you working for a supervisor or manager who is well-respected within the company and the industry?

If not, you may be in the wrong place for advancement. This creates a difficult position for you. Undermining an inefficient boss is lethal. Loyalty has a place. So, if you are working for someone who is not moving forward in his or her career, chances are that you will remain motionless, too. Choosing to move on to another position may be tough, but it may be your only hope of advancement.

Do you get along well with your boss?

Do you like him or her? If you don't, it is likely that your boss isn't crazy about you either. Self-evident, I expect. So, what are you waiting for? Move on out. A boss who doesn't like you won't promote you, however, you may easily ask for a transfer and get it. And who wants to stay where they're not liked?

Does your boss introduce you to his or her peers?

This is a sure sign that he or she acknowledges, respects, and trusts you. If you are dismissed from the conversation when another manager enters the room, notice this. You can, of course, be assertive. Once it is clear that you are not going to be introduced, you can make eye contact with the new person, walk towards them, extend your hand, and introduce yourself. Then, go about your normal duties. This takes gumption, but it clearly indicates your confidence. Folks will notice this.

When you are invited to join special meetings or task forces that others at your level are not, you can rest assured that you are on your way up. Indicate your interest and willingness to take on these responsibilities to your boss. She or he needs to know your blueprint, needs to know where you want to go. Enlist his/her help. When you do this, you are demonstrating respect for his or her ability to help you. Of course, every day you will have to clearly be doing everything in your power to demonstrate your competency to take that next step.

When your manager asks you to do things that are part of his or her job description, one of two things is true. You are being groomed, or, you are being used. You are being groomed when it demonstrates trust, reliance, and inclusion. You are being used when that trust and reliance is an effort to make you indispensable. *Remember, people who are indispensable in their current positions cannot be promoted.* Who would do the work as well? This would create an inconvenience for the manager and upheaval is not an exciting possibility.

How do you become dispensably indispensable?

Quietly train others to take over parts of your job while you actively seek to undertake parts of your boss' job. Then, when the time is right, you will be able to move forward seamlessly. You'll be applauded for your foresight and management ability.

OK, so these things are not happening where you work. Take a good look at the questions at the beginning of this topic. If you are not experiencing, or cannot envision experiencing, these things with your present company, manager, or supervisor, maybe you're in the wrong place to rise.

Assess things objectively. You may like the people but be stuck in place. There are great people everywhere. You may like the work but be stuck in place. There are other companies needing, wanting, even longing for competent people like you.

After careful assessment of the gap between your designed career path and your current career situation, it's time to decide. And, when in doubt, move on out!

**If you want to learn more about this assessment tool, contact info@optimizeinstitute.com.

WHEN THE WATERING HOLE SHRINKS. . .

As we've already discussed, when the watering hole shrinks, animals look at each other differently. That's the way it is at work when downsizing is occurring, too.

We look at each other differently. Our competitive natures rise to the forefront. Our suspicions about people's motives and behaviors pique. We watch for political moves. We become hyper-vigilant. Everything is a "sign." Watch out for this trend in your workplace.

> We must start with the reality that corporations cannot guarantee anyone a lifetime job any more than corporations have a guarantee of immortality.
>
> John Snow

You can only do the best possible job you can do. Be wise. Be pro-active. But, be assured that some things in the equation are entirely out of your control. *When you live each day in fear, you are paying attention to what you don't want.* Newsflash! **Paying attention to what you do not want attracts just that into your life.**

Does that sound simplistic? In fact, it is not. It is simple but profound.

- ✣ Who is in charge of your attitudes?
- ✣ Who is in charge of your sense of self?
- ✣ Who is in charge of your behavior? *Obviously, it's you.*
- ✣ What are you paying attention to?
- ✣ How is it affecting the quality of each day?

I was working with a coaching client who was obsessing about losing her job. At the beginning of the lay-offs, she had been twenty-fifth from the bottom of the list. Then one day she was fourth from the top—and with twenty-five years on the job. Naturally, she was concerned. And, she was at the top of her "what if?" game.

- ✣ What if I lose my job?
- ✣ What if the economy doesn't turn around?
- ✣ What if I can't get another job?
- ✣ What if I don't have the rent money?
- ✣ What if my relationship suffers?
- ✣ What will happen to my pension?

I didn't suggest there was no wisdom in keeping her eyes and ears open. I did not suggest she hide her head in the sand about the current conditions. What I did suggest was that her power was in her ability to keep the bigger picture in mind.

- ✣ Who was she?
- ✣ What were her strengths?
- ✣ How did she demonstrate what was important to her at work?
- ✣ What *could* she control and how could she exercise her options?

Fear causes folks to panic, to forget themselves. Normally pleasant, cooperative people clam up and keep their cards close to their chests. Outgoing people may talk more because they are anxious. Quiet folks may withdraw for the same reason. Fear exaggerates the negative in life. Don't let that happen. Get on top of it right now.

I'm talking about your *overall game plan in life.*

- ⊕ Make it as positive as you possibly can
- ⊕ Focus on what you want, where you're going and how you're going to get there
- ⊕ Make your conversation about what you want to attract into your life
- ⊕ Fill your mind with pictures of your ideal job, ideal relationships, ideal life

Only when you can clearly see the outcome you want are you likely to take a direct path to it. Remember that line from Lewis Carroll's *Alice in Wonderland*, "If you don't know where you're going, any path will take you there."

Know your destination and create your path. How does this translate to daily life at work when fear lurks? Again, your greatest choice every day is your attitude.

- ⊕ Where are you placing your energy?
- ⊕ How pro-active are you being?
- ⊕ Are you willing to ask questions that will help you make good choices and better plans?

Secrets seem to abound in workplaces that are dwindling. Some people are in the know, others are out of the loop. Ask questions. Get the facts.

**Be grounded in reality while steadfastly focused
on the outcome you want.**

If you believe in cooperation and collaboration, demonstrate it in the workplace consistently. Remember, whatever you value must be part of what you do and say every day, no matter what the climate or scenario. Don't be pulled off course from your beliefs and values by fear. Don't let the attitudes, fears and follies of others sway you from your path.

**Even if the lions are at the door, your best plan is to keep your
head. Be true to your values. Be pro-active.
And, definitely, don't feed them.**

IIIIIIIIIIIIIIIIIIIIIIIIIIIIIIIIIIIIIIIIIIIIIIIII Rhoberta Shaler, PhD IIIIIIIIIIIIIIIIIIIIIIIIIIIIIIIIIIIIIIIIIIIIIIIIIIIIII

**Do you work with your whole heart
and you will succeed—there is so little
competition.**

Elbert Hubbard

S

T

U

V

W

Y

Z

ABOUT THE AUTHOR

DR. RHOBERTA SHALER SOLVES "PEOPLE PROBLEMS" AT WORK. SHE MAKES IT EASIER TO TALK ABOUT DIFFICULT THINGS.

Dr. Shaler works with organizations that know their people are their top resource, and with leaders who know that building relationships is a top priority.

An expert facilitator, Dr. Shaler helps executives & entrepreneurs and their employees develop the effective communication skills needed to create powerful conversations that reduce conflict, build trust, and streamline negotiation.

Clients say that Rhoberta Shaler, PhD, is "a gentle, effective and enthusiastic teacher" who is "down-to-earth while knowledgeable, practical, energetic . . . and humorous." An acclaimed and popular keynote speaker, her light-hearted approach and value-packed content help audiences quickly grasp valuable skills & strategies. After more than twenty-five years in the business, Dr. Shaler continues to develop new programs to meet the needs of her clients and to meet the challenges she sees in the marketplace.

The Optimize! Institute founded by Dr. Shaler offers accessible executive & employee education to enhance communication and productivity, improve workplace relationships, manage conflict and build collaborative teams. With

Dr. Shaler's guidance, performance & profit improve in a more peaceful, dynamic culture.

Dr. Shaler was one of only eight original Premier Coaches across North America for eWomenNetwork and a founding member of the International Council of Online Professionals. Her PhD is in educational psychology, and her intensive training in all aspects of conflict management—negotiation, mediation, anger—was completed at the prestigious Justice Institute of British Columbia. She is the author of more than a dozen books & audio programs, as well as many manuals to improve specific people skills. Her books have been translated and published in Mexico, Taiwan, Latin America, Russia, China, Indonesia, and India. Her numerous articles are published in more than 17,000 web pages and 1000's of ezines around the world.

Dr. Shaler lives in Escondido, CA, has 3 adult children and 3 grandchildren. In her "me" time, she swims, practices yoga, shops for books, travels, and enjoys the company of friends.

Products available for you at
OptimizeInstitute.com

KEYNOTES, BOOKS, AUDIO PROGRAMS, TELESEMINARS, AND COACHING.

WRESTLING RHINOS
KEYNOTES, SEMINARS AND CORPORATE TRAINING

A rhino is an animal that simply cannot be ignored! No matter how you try to ignore, or deny, the presence of rhinos in your life, it simply will not work. If you don't wrestle the rhinos, both those inside yourself and those outside, you

will feel tense, anxious, off-balance, out of alignment and a little fragile. You might even feel like an impostor!

Dr. Shaler offers you the insights and strategies to name, claim, tame and lead away the rhinos that are getting in your way. Walk with her through the cages and savannahs of life and get tools and skills to wrestle the rhinos that stop you from progressing on the path to the goals, relationships, success and peace you desire. Available for corporations and communities. Book one today and start winning when wrestling rhinos!

Topics at www.OptimizeInstitute.com/keynotes

CORPORATE & COMMUNITY SEMINARS

For executives, entrepreneurs and employees, Dr. Shaler offers a complete range of people skills seminars on communication, conflict and anger management, and negotiation. The skills, insights and strategies offered in these seminars will increase peace, productivity and profits for you and your organization.

From conference breakouts to multi-day intensives, Dr. Shaler delivers practical, content-rich, in-depth training to make it easier to talk about difficult things. Bring her seminars to your office or community, or offer her teleseminars to your people. Provide your people with the high-level skills they need to solve people problems and learn to "play nicely together in the company sandbox" (or any sandbox). Seminars make a great value-added benefit for your clients, and really show that you're keeping their best interests at heart. Offer a *Wrestling Rhinos* component to your Board Retreat and get both the humor and skills to motivate and make a difference in your organization. Topics & details at www.OptimizeInstitute.com/seminars

---

OTHER BOOKS, AUDIO PROGRAMS, TELESEMINARS

OPTIMIZE YOUR DAY! PRACTICAL WISDOM FOR OPTIMAL LIVING.

This beautiful 6x6 book makes a terrific gift, coffee table book or even bathroom book! You'll find motivational quotes, thoughts and insights to change your day and your life. There is space for you to keep a journal as well.

KEEP IT IN MIND: MEMORABLE MESSAGES FOR STAYING ON TRACK.

Just when you thought the detours seemed endless, Dr. Rhoberta Shaler draws you a simple map for the road to success. Avoid tempting parking places. Remove roadblocks. Straightforward, practical wisdom to enhance your life.

WHAT YOU PAY ATTENTION TO EXPANDS: FOCUS YOUR THINKING.

Change Your Results. This book is filled with the fuel to kickstart your success! Open yourself to the world of positive thought and personal accountability with these easy-to-apply concepts that will rev your engine and take you where you want to go. (Also available in Spanish)

AUDIO PROGRAM: WRESTLING RHINOS—CONQUERING CONFLICT IN THE WILDS OF WORK

Get the 1-hour audio program based on this book.

AUDIO PROGRAM: CONFLICT IS NOT A 4-LETTER WORD.

Managing conflict can be a tricky and delicate job. These two insightful audio seminars will give you proven strategies for resolving conflicts successfully - and creating healthy relationships - at work and at home. On 2 CDs.

AUDIO PROGRAM: CREATING YOUR LIFE

Includes three of Dr. Shaler's most popular talks: You Are the Mastermind of Your Masterpiece, Be Positively Selfish and Be A Real Goal Getter! This series of seminars WILL motivate you to keep on track. On 2 CDs

AUDIO PROGRAM: YOUR PAST IS NOT YOUR POTENTIAL

Get motivated to give yourself permission to MOVE ON! Allowing your past mistakes and regrets to hold you back from future success is a common stumbling block for millions of people. Learn how to let to, and "get on with it!"

AUDIO PROGRAM: HOW TO MAKE AN ENTRANCE & WORK A ROOM

Dr. Shaler's popular Power Networking seminar on CD. These tips, techniques, insights and proven strategies will give you the knowledge necessary to walk confidently into any new setting or relationship and know that you will be remembered for the RIGHT reasons.

AUDIO PROGRAM: PROSPERITY ON PURPOSE™

Rhoberta Shaler, PhD presents Prosperity on Purpose™: Eight Essentials for Living Richly in Every Way. This 8-CD set gives you the insights, inspiration and information you need to shift your results from acceptable to exceptional, in every area of life.

1-HOUR CRASH COURSES (TELESEMINARS)

Teleseminars bring the skills, insights & strategies you need to grow your business, strengthen your team, or improve your life—directly to you on the telephone. There are fourteen teleseminars available on a wide range of important and necessary topics to help you solve your "people problems" and develop your skill set.

CONTACT US FOR CUSTOMIZED KEYNOTES, SEMINARS, AND TELESEMINARS

WWW.OPTIMIZEINSTITUTE.COM

INFO@OPTIMIZEINSTITUTE.COM

760.735.8686

CPSIA information can be obtained at www.ICGtesting.com
Printed in the USA
BVOW05s1832080514

352822BV00002B/660/A

9 780971 168985